Michael Hampton

Unshelfmarked
Reconceiving the artists' book

Uniformbooks 2015

The author and publisher gratefully acknowledge the following for permission to reproduce material used in this book: p.14: Steve Clay, Granary Books and Johanna Drucker; p.23: Erica Van Horn, Simon Cutts; p.29: Victoria Browne; p.33: Michael Tompert/Paul Fairchild, Rex Features; p.37: Ronald King, Circle Press; p.49: Courtesy of The John Latham Foundation and Lisson Gallery (photo: Ken Adlard); p.99: Linda Toigo; p.113: Guy Begbie; p.121: Nigel Slight; p.125: Sarah Bodman; p.135: Vito Drago, England & Co.; p.141: Courtesy of Brian Dettmer and P.P.O.W Gallery, New York; p.145: Alan Loney; p.153: Christina Mitrentse; p.155: Ruth Beale.

First published 2015

ISBN 978-1-910010-06-8

Uniformbooks
7 Hillhead Terrace, Axminster, Devon EX13 5JL
www.uniformbooks.co.uk

Trade distribution in the UK by Central Books
www.centralbooks.com

Printed and bound by T J International, Padstow, Cornwall

"It is interesting to contemplate an entangled bank, clothed with many plants of many kinds, with birds singing on the bushes, with various insects flitting about, and with worms crawling through the damp earth, and to reflect that these elaborately constructed forms, so different from each other, and dependent on each other in so complex a manner, have all been produced by laws acting around us."

— Charles Darwin, *The Origin of Species* (1859)

Contents

Foreword

Of late, libraries everywhere are publishing books highlighting their printed and manuscript 'Treasures'. Notwithstanding that many of the works included may be illustrated online, perhaps more extensively, and for free, there remains a market for the instructive pleasure of browsing such curated selections, well printed and with authoritative and engaged commentaries. The book in hand has something in common with such compilations, though its plums —Prehistoric, Medieval, Renaissance and from each later century— would have to be abstracted from several top-class collections to realise this fantasy library. The popularity of these and other books about books owes much to the emergence, this last half-century, of book history as an academic, interdisciplinary vortex out of textual criticism, printing history, sociology, media studies and art history. The same period birthed the idea of book art and the term 'artists' books'.

The classic titles and bibliographic artefacts selected here are interspersed among a greater number of works produced since the 1960s, mainly by artists. Almost half of these date from the present century, which has seen a renewed surge of artists using bibliographic formats, modes and tropes, despite, and/or in active relation to, the various digital transformations now overtaking existing bibliographic arrangements. Naturally, fewer of these recent works have yet attained 'treasure' status, unlike either the de luxe *livres d'artistes* of the earlier 20th century, Russian Futurist publications or the work of Surrealist artists, although certain of them have some celebrity.

Shelfmarking generally manifests classification, the grouping and sequencing of books on library shelves, supposed to help the browsing reader who (it is assumed) shares the librarian's preference for like with like. Not every library adopts this principle. Some store purely by size: it saves time, it saves space (it does at least reveal the order in which items were acquired) and a shelfmark still assigns a book a permanent home—it can be discovered, delivered, and audited. But probably no-one browses that shelf.

This book is an intentional act of *un*-shelfmarking, freed from constraints of collection management, access and accountability. The randomness of alphabetical listing reveals similarities among approaches to the book space at different periods and to ostensibly quite different ends. Typologies, moveable parts, commentary, visual text and self-reflexive games as well as annotation, alteration and collage are among the formal and generic analogues.

New links and likenesses are stimulating, but are they significant? The highest duty of both books and readers is to produce meaning. Artists' books at best are *books*. They have information for us. They expose. They can be critical, and political. They turn over ideas, including ideas about the book itself; they are cybernetic, and they play. You can lose and find yourself in a book. Some poetry will out.

The great service of this commentated bibliography is to discover that the experience of artists' books encourages *the art of reading*: a rich, productive reception, such as people perform in their gallery-going. With minds and sensors thus attuned, why would you not turn the same attention outward and backwards, to the whole world of books: the texts and depictions that have been instantiated and promulgated in portable visual and material formats? The categorical ladder falls away.

Elizabeth James
Senior Librarian
National Art Library, V&A Museum

Unshelfmarked

In retrospect, the goal of identifying with any degree of chronological accuracy the moment a specific project begins is difficult, since the mental processes or 'project narrative' which always underpin and convey such tasks themselves have no clear cut beginning or end, and so this preamble is itself a cross-section.

My interest in the phenomenon of the artists' book and the vexed issue of how to re-conceptualise it has slowly taken the place of an earlier intellectual engagement that focused on destruction in post-war art. However, both the issue (by which I mean the sometimes caustic debate over identity) and extended reach of the artists' book hasn't led to any neat therapeutic resolution or synthesis of the crisis in art that found its voice and form from the early 1960s, through a range of by now well documented shocking actions that marked art's emancipation from what Hans Haacke has called a

> "...secluded and holy sphere".[1]

This is because en route the book itself has often been reduced to a crude object, depersonalised almost, in order to speed its break down into cellular components, or as a necessary prelude to its re-emergence as a sophisticated designer object; so many types of material rebirth, or what the market brands 'product innovation'.

> "...specific media are staging areas for the warping and weaving of the process of semiosis across forms, genres and non-artistic disciplines."[2]

Therefore it would be mistaken to pile utopian value onto the form and mission of the historical artists' book,[3] or be misled by the red herring of its fundamental identity.[4] However, to speak of the artists' book as if solely a quirky Cinderella-like branch of the six hundred year-old history of the book as codex, or even a late-capitalist symptom, would be to ignore the impact of the digital revolution upon it too, a seismic event that has coincided with its structural renewal and expansion, revealing a fluid, highly adaptable and above all democratic format in the process. The page-based artists' book, it turned out, had been in waiting for electronic pixellation all along.[5]

From the autumn of 2009 I was asked by Victoria Browne to contribute to Kaleid Editions, a publishing project and bookshop based in Shoreditch, London E2, and spent my office time there under the pseudonym Redchurch Idler writing extremely compressed or 'flash' reviews of new work commissioned by the space.[6] The very first show at the unit, Leigh Clarke's 'Our Worlds Collided' included the eponymous *Our Worlds Collided* (2009), a series of photocopied latex masks, laminated and bound in a lever arch file. My response to it was scarcely discursive, owing more to the conventions of Cambridge L=a=n=g=u=a=g=e poetry

> "Babyfaced/squashed/écrasé/flattened/punctured/
> mashed/comminuted/warped/flayed/anonymised/
> trashed/defaced/plasticated/mutilated/crumpled/
> stigmatised/abominated/KO'ed/Mercatored/
> snagged/debased/anamorphised/scarified/chewed/
> dirempted/bashed/framed/unidentified/abused/
> pulped/compacted/deflated/bodged/knackered/
> layered/embalmed/roadkilled/Torquemada'ed/kaput/
> vandalised/mullered/undercarded/bastardised/
> demonised/dissed/shrinkwrapped/cameoed/twisted/
> deadbeaten/rammed/1D'ed/scrunched/crushed/
> Metzgered/guineapigged/remixed/outlasted/JCB'ed/
> Oldboyed/soft-targeted."

But the point is made, namely that the vestiges of Clarke's unethical sessions over a photocopy machine constituted the work, this stabbing review a link between the domains of destruction in art and the artists' book. As it turned out, at Kaleid Editions both the amount and diversity of new work specially developed over the next year and a half of its tenure in Redchurch Street would be remarkable, a snapshot of contemporary goings-on in the ever expanding world of the artists' book, true to the project's subtitle and mission statement "artists who do books"—with all the under and overtones you could handle packed into that small lower-case Ruscha verb "do". Highlights of the programme were *Designed by Fraser Muggeridge Studio* (2010), a volume of forty-eight handbound books which I described as

> "The product of secret disbinding by an assistant with hot iron and paring knife, *Designed by Fraser Muggeridge Studio* is not just a crafty way to showcase a back catalogue, but hints at a darker agenda: of interbreeding, and recombinance, explicit messing with bibliographic protocols."

Memorable too were Jonathan Ward's *Little Wonder* (2010), a limited edition album with a selection of laser cut tea cards, Helen Schoene's performance *Hairpiece* (2010), and an exuberant pre-Christmas group show *The Grand Plasto-Baader-Books*, that referenced the Dadaist Johannes Baader's infamous 1920 bricolage. My analysis of this event found its way into the pages of *The Blue Notebook*,[7] a journal which accompanies the bi-monthly electronic *Book Arts Newsletter*, also run by Sarah Bodman from the Centre for Fine Print Research at the University of the West of England, Bristol. The *BAN* (wisely eschewing the term 'artists' book' in its title) opened my eyes to a diversity of work, working methods, exhibitions, opportunities, hands-on courses, interactive projects and conferences, functioning as a parish-pump newspaper as well as gauge of contemporary book arts world-wide, not to mention an incremental archive of this rapidly evolving domain, a Great Barrier Reef of shimmering life-forms.

Towards the end of 2010 I was galvanised by one of the many opportunities posted on *BAN*, an open invitation call by MAK, the Austrian Museum of Applied Arts, to set about making a new piece of work for ABOT, or 'Artists' Books on Tour', the projected ports of call being in Vienna at the Contemporary Art Library and Works on Paper Collection at Stubenring 5, Prague and Ljubljana, the terminus for this mobile museum. I submitted an album,

> "A specially written theoretical cover mounted text and 29 entries tipped-in to a plain photo album 16 x 21cm, this work is low on ornamentation and high on conceptual content.
>
> Designed as a direct response to the ABOT project brief, which like many short histories of the so-called artists' book seems to be limited both in its historical scope and definition, i.e. that the artists' book began with William Blake, *THEARTISTSBOOKANEWHISTORY* attempts to blow open the question of the artists' book both by expanding the 'canon' retrospectively to the Stone Age, and also by linking the 20th century efflorescence of the form to the radical multimedia art movement VORTICISM.
>
> *THEARTISTSBOOKANEWHISTORY* is also a work-in-progress, and the album submitted here the initial prototype, as the list of works printed on the pink slips is NOT final, but evidence of an dynamic act of historical revisionism in a fast moving era when technology is leading to the wholesale breaking down of cultural categories, and the sudden emergence of a brand new transdisciplinarity.
>
> From a research perspective there is something for everyone here, as each of the 29 entries is a starting point in itself, inviting the reader/user to explore the pathway opened up in time and space by each work quoted."

Naturally the tactic of challenging a given frame of reference in your supporting statement is a risky one (albeit highly productive here) since such a manoeuvre can also be read as a covert attack on the autonomy and authority of the institution that has laid down those parameters. Perhaps I was courting rejection, irritated by that over confident sentence in MAK's brief sanctifying William Blake's *The Marriage of Heaven and Hell* (1790–93).

> "The history of artists' books, almost two centuries long, is informed by ongoing research of the medium and its mutations. The beginnings of the genre can be identified in William Blake's *The Marriage of Heaven and Hell* and *Songs of Innocence and of Experience* in which Blake's approach to text and images differed from that otherwise used in illustrated books. He created the prototype of what came to be known as the artist's book."

This privileging of Blake's DIY practice is a simplistic one that has enabled a generic model to be built from ground zero. Blake's hybridised practice has literally been locked in on the side of the artists' book, providing the alleged source of its difference and deviance, causing Johanna Drucker to wax lyrical about

> "His capacity to mobilise the space of the page, the tones of the paper, the colours of ink and paint, to perform a drama of monumental proportions within the relatively small scale of his books, demonstrates an understanding of the book's communicative power. The independent spaces of text and image exist in a dialogic relationship to each other, often losing their autonomy in the interlacing of border motifs with the letters of the text, the drawn form of the regular, small writing imbued with a liveliness of touch which invariably resonates with the sinews of line which inscribe the visual forms of image."[8]

and

> "Expanding and shrinking against the finite edges of the page, the elements of the whole turn inward for their definition, performing as the basic elements of a replete cosmos of thought."[9]

Finally 925 projects were whittled down to 158, from which the five winners were selected. My album of tipped-in titles not being among these, I joked to myself this was a rejection by the Viennese art establishment of Hitlerian proportions.

> "You can see how a sensitive, brooding individual who feels he has been shortchanged in the Vienna swap-shop, begins to torture himself with the dead old question of why bother? Merely to carve a scar on the universe."[10]

After a brief period of disillusionment with the project, I emailed some images of the album to Ami Clarke, a design artist and founder of Banner Repeater, a project space, reading room and archive located on platform 1 of Hackney Downs railway station, east London.[11] Beginning from a mutual interest in Vorticism, in the spring of 2011 she encouraged me to carry on, both by expanding the treatise and adding considerably to the original list. My initial flamboyant act of historical revisionism was now set to become a studied thesis, a discussion document which, it must be admitted, apart from one or two exceptions has failed to provoke much, perhaps because its thrust threatens the distinctive coteries and contagious clubs that have built up in the realm of the artists' book?

Finally the speculative text and long list were combined and published as *THEARTISTSBOOKANEWHISTORY*.[12] Its binary format owed a subliminal debt to Germano Celant's *Book as Artwork 1960/1972* (1972), ostensibly a catalogue bracing together an essay and bibliographic list, although Celant was modest in his claim that

> "This essay and list are necessarily incomplete, as they attempt to be a first analysis of books as artworks."[13]

This statement conveys an almost elegiac sense of deficit, of work still to be done as well as a challenge to the near future, not to say impossibility of ever doing justice to the field of investigation, a state of affairs that has grown ever more critical since the early 1970s; so much so in fact that Celant's adoption of the list[14] seems prescient from the standpoint of 2015, an era in which information overload is the norm, and listing the dominant mental form of data management and compression.

THEARTISTSBOOKANEWHISTORY was produced as a fold-out leaflet[15] in a run of 500 by the not-for-profit Banner Repeater in November 2011, and distributed for free via the station bookstall with the logistical aplomb of W. H. Smith. During the natural course of its dispersal, one response from publisher Colin Sackett proved to be decisive for *Unshelfmarked: Reconceiving the Artists' Book*, this latest manifestation of a big idea: the Mk III version. Sackett's invitation in the spring of 2012 to overhaul and expand *THEARTISTSBOOKANEWHISTORY* into a book-length publication was a significant challenge.

Reinventing the title alone has been a drawn-out heuristic process, but the new version *Unshelfmarked*, a title Sackett has declared himself "...very enamoured with" (email, 27 February 2013) indicates a subtle conceptual difference from the earlier head-on attack, a de facto weighing up, and elaboration. Baconian in scope, the research project's original form, a binary structure of list and theoretical text, has been kept and expanded, then conjoined with an appendix and a specialised reference bibliography designed for users, makers and literati of the artists' book.

So what is it about the list, and its modern variant, the Listopia or BuzFeed listicle that is quite so irresistible as a format? A shopping list scrawled on the back of an envelope is throwaway, but possesses the key working features of any and all lists, i.e. their portability, brevity and handiness. In short, the list is often the first line of organisational defence in the battle with the incomprehensibility and furor of daily life in 2015; an unbeatable memory device.

Shaun Usher's book *Lists of Note* (2014), selects 125 celebrity lists through time that function variously as do's and don'ts, rules and etiquette, predictions, lexicons, even suspect lists. But Umberto Eco's *The Infinity of Lists* (2009) raises the bar of analysis to show how the list as *enumeratio*, congeries, *incrementum*, climax, gradation and panegyric was a nuanced way of ordering fundamentally disordered sets of items, thereby explicitly linking its purpose to the art of wonderment, and thus early modern *wunderkammern* themselves.

In *Unshelfmarked* the list is one that taxonomises cultural evidence, dealing economically with a vast pile up, which is enlisted to buttress a series of conclusions about the artists' book, bearing in mind Eco's observation:

> "A practical list is never incongruous, provided we can identify the criterion of assembly that governs it."[16]

But discerning that criterion is a job for the reader, although by itself insufficient, for the intriguing resonances emitted by the list in *Unshelfmarked* depend to an extent on chance, in so far as its alphabetic logic has generated some unlikely syntactical juxtapositions, and equally striking chronological differences. Aggregating works normally viewed as phenomenologically far apart from each other evokes the Renaissance *studiolo*, a scholarly rather than academic space, a matrix where natural wonders co-mingled with artificial ones, e.g. conch shells besides scalpels, vegetable lambs next to pilgrim badges; a semi-delirious research facility.

And what does *Unshelfmarked* mean, this odd word which is certainly not in any dictionary worth its salt? Closely allied with the term de-accessioned, it describes a potential process whereby certain ancient artefacts or "book-like thingies" (see Exposé), as well as a range of post-Gutenberg printed texts whose cataloguing within a bibliographic system is taken for granted, are either seen as chronically unsuitable for shelfmarking or conceptually de-classed, estranged, and removed from the dominant epistemological shadow or hold of an institutional method of ordering, even if inside the rarified space of Special Collections. Thus the title *Unshelfmarked* functions as an epithet announcing a promissory suspension, one which visualises the art of individual as opposed to institutional collection to be the result of unique personal choice typified by the amassing of seemingly miscellaneous materials, i.e. the para-library contained in these pages.

Many of the items finally populated as a list here would previously have been viewed as belonging to a realm well beyond the one circumscribed under the heading Artists' Book, statistical outliers so to speak.[17] My trick sets this 'dark flow'[18] of inter-galactic objects free, disobliging them to make sense according to the logic of a mere substitutive system. Post-Deweyed, these works form an entirely new corpus, showcasing the artists' book not as a by-product of the book *per se*, but both its antecedent and post-digital flowering, many salient twentieth-century features proleptically flickering here and there through time, its epigenetic influence finally come to permeate mainstream book design everywhere; the manifold traits and studio processes inherent to the artists' book bursting from their stitched sheath, cheerfully pollinating the whole gamut of reading impedimenta and spaces.

Michael Hampton
Battersea, 2015

Notes

1 www.sfmoma.org/explore/multimedia/videos/679

2 John Roberts, *The Intangibilities of Form* (London/New York, NY: Verso, 2007), p.14.

3 The website of the 4th Sheffield International Artists' Book Prize contained this lapidary statement: "We have no desire to engage in discussion about what constitutes an artist's book beyond clarifying that the prize is not concerned with books about art or artists, but books as art." www.artistsbookprize.co.uk

4 Which Elizabeth James has called "… the pestiferous issue of definitions" (email, 14 December 2014).

5 For more on the effect of digital technologies upon the interdisciplinary book, see Emmanuelle Waeckerlé & Richard Sawdon Smith (eds.), *The Book is Alive!* (2013).

6 Reviews may be read at www.kaleideditions.com

7 *The Blue Notebook*, vol.4, no.2, April 2010.

8 Johanna Drucker, *The Century of Artists' Books* (1995) p.25.

9 Ibid., p.25.

10 Paul West, *The Dry Danube: A Hitler Forgery* (New York, NY: New Directions Books, 2000), p.91.

11 www.bannerrepeater.org

12 Characterised as "fictocriticism" in a review by Ajay Hothi. www.bookarts.uwe.ac.uk/pdf/newspdfs/80.pdf

13 The tone of this remark is suggestive of Friedrich Schlegel's anti-foundationalist romantic philosophy, which *in media res* embraced the fragmentary, uncertain, vertiginous and *unendlich*.

14 Celant, *Book as Artwork 1960/1972* (1972) p.3.

15 I am indebted to Ami Clarke for the idea of interpolating its diagonal searchlights, textual material lifted verbatim from Wyndham Lewis's *Blast* (1914).

16 Umberto Eco, *The Infinity of Lists* (London: MacLehose Press, 2009), p.116.

17 For example, to conservative eyes, including Urbanomic in the following treasury may look hare-brained and implausible, but no more so than the presence of *Landry M'Batu Cretan Spirals*, 1600 BC, in the original leaflet! Nevertheless re-conceiving a twitter feed as a meta-book is in line with the underlying thrust of *Unshelfmarked*: which is to look again at the familiar and defamiliarise it, whilst re-invigorating what had been thought to be a canonic set or closed shop through challenging its membership criteria, and establishing a brand new historical timeline too.

18 Term borrowed from particle physics which describes the still to be accounted for effects of dark matter.

“The list relies on discontinuity rather than continuity; it depends on physical placement, on location; it can be read in different directions, both sideways and downwards, up and down, as well as left and right; it has a clear-cut beginning and a precise end, that is, a boundary, an edge, like a piece of cloth.”

—Jack Goody, *The Domestication of the Savage Mind* (1977)

About Two Squares

El Lissitzky, 1922
—wire-stitched newsprint, letterpress

Dedicated TO ALL CHILDREN TO ALL CHILDREN, this Cyrillic re-iteration on the first page of El Lissitzky's Suprematist tour-de-force *About Two Squares* metaphorically addresses Soviet workers, or the children of the Bolshevik revolution (he had been working on *About Two Squares* at Kasimir Malevich's experimental art school in Vitebsk since 1920), a subset of all humanity. Unregenerate society still labouring in darkness under international capitalism was represented in this 'tale' by a black square, communism needless to say by the blood red, destined to rejuvenate the oppressed mass of humankind in an emblematic victory of one seraphic shape over the other diabolical one.

The scientific romance depicted in *About Two Squares* relies on the absolutely new way El Lissitzky combines typography and images, giving them equal valency. The injunction DON'T READ is supplemented by advice: TAKE PAPER COLUMNS BLOCKS and FOLD COLOUR BUILD. Such ground rules, laid down with boundless confidence, enable the six constructions upon which the fable is based to be realised in an extraordinary burst of non-objective dynamism. We are a million miles away here from the late medieval practices of William Morris's Kelmscott Press, for the techniques piloted in *About Two Squares* might plausibly be seen as the elemental precursors for both the style and methodology of the 20th century artists' book in general.

El Lissitzky cut his teeth as a designer/editor and underlined his Cubo-Futurist credentials in *About Two Squares* through a giddying adherence to and application of the point, the plane and the line, taking an architectural approach to art rather than one derived from the easel, with all its phenomenological limitations. He extended the conceptual reach of Malevich's PROUN, or Projects for the Affirmation of the New, which while being of necessity pedagogic in scope, remained joyfully destructive. The restless geometrical narrative concludes optimistically with the settling down of the red square on top of the black, and with the quasi-Biblical HERE IT ENDED. But of course in the Suprematist multiverse nothing ever really ends, and *About Two Squares* is just a portal, a chamber through which packets of verbal energy and disintegrating forms whiz, spin and for a fleeting moment miraculously create their own strange order.

In *About Two Squares* El Lissitzky championed diagonal typesetting, inducing that cosmic vertigo we must repress in order to survive, since it is with us 24/7, despite the banal grid of straight lines and static represented forms which underpin the illusion of reality.

Airmail Envelope Interiors

Erica Van Horn & Simon Cutts, 2002
—laser print, letterpress, offset

Purged of informational and sentimental content, i.e. the letters they once contained, these samples of faded denim blue for the most part convey not only absence but also historical contingency, as the distinctive aeroplane logo many of the paper interiors bear occurs as a feint petroglyph; rock art of a distant civilisation to be decoded by ethnographers in millenia to come, owing their beauty to the implication they have been cut out from one huge surrealist sheet; intercontinental epistolary wrapping paper.

Yet the very speed of 21st century global communications makes the concept of a 75gsm airmail envelope, either the all-in-one self-seal format or traditional envelope with red & blue chevron border, appear almost as quaint as Phileas Fogg's balloon. The bank of company acronyms SAS KLM PANAM AIR CANADA IRISH stamped on one page seems equally fragile in the current climate of aggressive corporate takeovers and mergers.

How though to read a publication such as *Airmail Envelope Interiors*? Well, reading is perhaps a wrongheaded response and viewing a much more apt mode, since both its texture and scope is painterly. Cutts helps us out:

> "The presence of the book is invitational. The individual reader opens the closed pages in an intimate setting. The book reveals its sensation as it is unfolded at a pace controlled by the reader."[1]

Interaction with *Interiors* is as if with the inside track of a Möbius strip, the back of a painting or the underside of a piece of shagreen, an enfolding skin held up to the light and appreciated for its own sake, an overlooked marvel made all the more marvellous since the art of collecting such neo-Merz is an unofficial, even absurd pastime compared with the serious business of stamp or vintage postcard collecting. The artists' book can accommodate such trifles however: not fundamentally a technical guide-book, encyclopaedia or site of scientific analysis, and in this instance the home-made record of a perfectly legitimate infatuation with airmail envelopes.

The Victorians would adorn wooden fireplace screens and other household objects with *découpage*, but Van Horn and Cutts, by preserving a few ragged specimens of the scrap, the off-cut, the ort, demonstrate intra rather than extra-illustration, removing the pith from the pith helmet so to speak; flying us in the cheap seats.

1 Simon Cutts, 'The Process of the Book: Address to the Art Education Association of Western Australia, Perth 1980', *Some Forms of Availability* (Derby: RGAP, 2007), p.57.

Anonyme Skulpturen
A Typology of Technical Constructions

Bernhard & Hilla Becher, 1970
—gelatin silver photographs, offset

With a quick snap of their fingers, sundry grain elevators, coal bunkers, lime kilns, storage sheds and water towers were declared to be 'anonymous sculpture', an extraordinarily clever conceptual act of denomination, and key to understanding the work of the Bechers', married photographers based in Düsseldorf, who became best known for their typological collections of industrial buildings. Yet the hardcore term itself derived from the second issue of a short-lived German art magazine.[1]

Dominated by the grim full-frontal view, with an occasional foray into more oblique perspectives, disinterested in weather,[2] and purged of any Friedrichesque human staffage, the monolithic credentials of the utilitarian buildings examined by the Bechers' lens emerge from their formal treatment of these sites. Yet such withering detachment grows suspicious at times, as if a fully functional therapeutic shield erected against recall of the near Nazi past, since their wide-ranging oeuvre contains no images of concentration camp gas chambers or decaying crematoria, flatness less an aesthetic, than evidence of numb inadequacy.

The Bechers' grammatical style has had a widespread influence, particularly upon the mordant narrative voice of Patrick Keiller's films *Robinson in Space* (1997) and *Robinson in Ruins* (2010), in which buildings are regarded as indexical found objects. Becherism also informs the deadpan English Home Counties manner favoured by architectural critic Jonathan Meades, whose televisual brand of faux-Teutonic commentary is precisely the sort of maverick licence the couple couldn't ever have allowed themselves.

Since many of the muscular edifices were awaiting demolition and the scrapyard, these behemoths of a heavy industrial past about to be superseded either by new and cleaner technologies, or the re-location of their manufacturing processes to Third World countries with lower wage costs, stand today as sombre reminders of European built heritage, and thanks to the Bechers' 'anonymous sculpture' which didn't vanish without trace.

As photobook, the design of *Anonyme Skulpturen* can border on sterility, but such a value judgement is made in the light of an explosive growth and diversification of the form, as user-friendly 21st century digital technology makes publishing available to all,[3] while the grungy code of urban exploration inspired by such texts as the late Jeff Chapman's *Access All Areas* (2005) and RomanyWG's *Beauty in Decay* (2012) favours a conservationist approach to trespass, or 'place hacking' inside ruins rather than eyeing them as façade dominated statues.[4]

---

1 *Kunst-Zeitung*, no.2, January 1969.

2 In his review of 'Bernd and Hilla Becher', Sonnabend Gallery, New York, 2012, Ara H. Merjian notes how "The same inexorably milky sky frames each structure, and atmospheric indicators are so minimal as to compel concentration upon the objects themselves." *Artforum*, December 2012.

3 For example Craig Atkinson's Café Royal imprint, an ongoing series of A5 photobooks that document social change in Britain. His own multi-view *Preston Bus Station Up and Over* (2014), attempts to identify the stunning if somewhat shabby grandeur of this Grade II Listed modernist icon.

4 uk.news.yahoo.com/photos/secret-tourist-spots-18-hauntingly-beautiful-pictures-of-abandoned-buildings-1394462559-slideshow/

Barents Lessons
Teaching and Research in Architecture

Harry Gugger, Nancy Couling, Aurélie Blanchard (eds.), 2012
—infographics, illustration, maps, offset

To receive an award isn't always a mark of excellence. Sometimes it is just the result of excessive networking, or a lack of critical oversight. In the case of *Barents Lessons* though, that was recognised as one of the twenty Most Beautiful Swiss Books of 2012, the accolade, bestowed every year by the rather forbiddingly named Swiss Federal Office of Culture, is well earned.

Its graphics and applied methodology elide perfectly (rendering it 'beautiful'), and this raises it a bit above the already quite high production standards of most geography texts. As a series of lessons, it has a dynamic effect, introducing the little known Barents Sea area to potential readers, thereby announcing the Arctic region almost as a new player and, as Greenpeace will attest, hazardous eco-battleground in 21st century geopolitics.

Carried out by masters students as a one year investigation, *Barents Lessons* is divided up into three sections: Analysis, Field Trip and Architectural Projects, with the blend of long distance surveillance and close up report represented via fold-out maps, charts, architectural schematics and zoological drawings. This rich mix of infographic content, organised by the physical separation of the three parts via tabs, makes for a heightened reading experience.

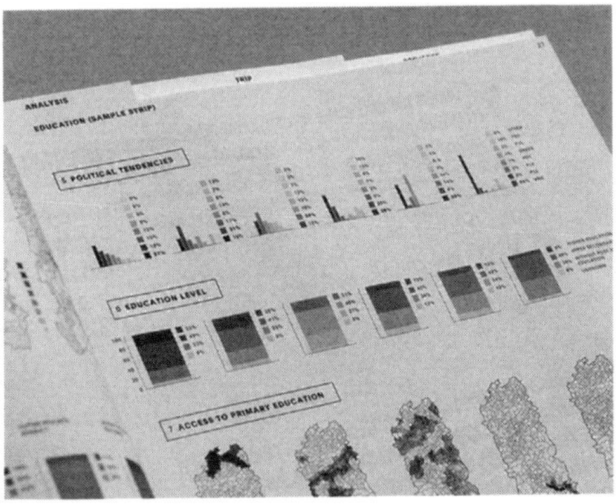

Perhaps the greatest achievement of *Barents Lessons*, though, is to grab hold of your attention and keep it, which when set against the immaterial flux, distraction and engulfing power of our multi-platform mediasphere, says much about the informational presentation and visual appeal of a publication ostensibly resembling a plain textbook. But it is in fact the vehicle of both a complex conceptual space, and also by means of its futuristic proposals for development, an important documentary resource and warning beacon for those invisible businessmen who see such 'unspoilt' offshore zones as the Baring Sea as little more than fossil fuel resources to drill out and leave behind depleted and sad, without giving any heed to the wider impact of their predatory operations.

Between Artificial Flowers & Asbestos Removal

Victoria Browne, 2013

—laser print

Devised for the group show 'Unending',[1] and adopting the advertising formats commonly found in Yellow Pages duly laid out as a double-page spread, Victoria Browne skilfully parodies the runaway careerist self-promotion[2] that has become the new norm in the world of contemporary art, as simultaneously she indulges in a plug for her own printmaking.[3] We can choose between '24hr Immediate Response', 'Sweet Success', 'Printmaker Direct' or 'Essex Artist' with sales straplines such as 'All Areas Covered', 'Original Quality Prints for Special Occasions', 'Established Over 35 Years' (i.e. her age), and even learn via a serious small print insert about how she

> "…draws on public special collections to appropriate material research, applying traditional and innovative print techniques in the development of site specific installations".

This send-up of trade means that *Between Artificial Flowers & Asbestos Removal* avoids the po-facedness of much textually-based conceptual art. Fast call out, customer convenience and bulk discounting are just some of lures of a dog-eat-dog marketplace that Browne has cottoned on to for her own absurdist ends, even as a long list of services that includes etching, linoleum cut, polymergravure, screenprint and stone lithograph make it clear that the artist's motives are strictly professional. Phone number, personal website, email and business address drive it all home too, giving a brand new twist to the task of thumbing through a directory and ringing round for the best quote on a job.

Inserting a phoney ad in a newspaper or magazine isn't new, and was explored by early conceptual artists such as Cildo Meireles in

Insertions into Ideological Circuits, 1970, whilst latterly to promote MI!MS, Andy Holden has rented the advertising cover of his local paper *Bedford Times & Citizen*, as indeed have Division of Labour, a project space whose ongoing commissioning project 'Est. 1690', generates a regular wrap for allegedly the world's oldest local newspaper *Berrow's Worcester Journal*.[4] But Browne's over-the-top *feuilleton* takes the biscuit: designed to be temporarily slipped into a library's supply of soon to be obsolete printed directories,[5] it mocks a topsy-turvy Alice world, whose blanket virality and venality have become inseparable, Tweedledee going absolutely everywhere with Tweedledum.

1 'Unending', Westminster Reference Library, London, 24 June–26 July 2014. The vertiginous title of this group exhibition was cropped from Jorge Luis Borges's observation in the short story 'The Library of Babel', that "...the library is unending".

2 According to Browne, *Between Artificial Flowers & Asbestos Removal* "...came about due to the pressure to sign up to online social media" (email, 24 Febuary 2014). A final limited edition of ten, comprising a copy of *Yellow Pages* and the insert housed in a handmade box with hot foil blocking is due to be published by Kaleid Editions in 2015.

3 This should be compared with its polar opposite: the deliberate concealment practised by the homonymically named (sic) Stanley Brouwn. Since 1972, every catalogue or group exhibition the Surinam born artist has participated in, comes with the qualification "At the request of the artist there are no photos or bio-bibliographical data" or "At the artist's request, his birth date is excluded here, and the works are not reproduced", or some conceptual variation thereof.

4 See my report 'Est. 1690: Read All About It', *Art Monthly*, no.370, November 2013.

5 Christian Boltanski's *The Inhabitants of Malmö* (1994), consisted of a sticker for the front page of the city's telephone directory plus a four page errata slip subtitled *You cannot reach these inhabitants of Malmö on the phone anymore. They died in 1993.*

The Birds of America

J. J. Audubon, 1827–1839
—etching, aquatint, watercolour, letterpress

MISCELLANEOUS ORNITHOLOGY NOTES or Audubon *ekphrasis*:
i. American Avocet (*Recurviostra americana*): long upturned beak ajar to probe the sandy foreshore. ii. Barnacle Geese (*Branta leucosis*): vociferous doglike honkers. iii. Delafield's Ground Warbler (*Sylvia Delafieldii*): not to be confused with the Common Yellowthroat. iv. American Flamingo (*Phoenicopterus ruber*): pink body hinged at the neck to wet its large bill. v. American Goldfinch (*Carduelis tristis*): perched daintily on flowering thistle heads. vi. Brown Noddy (*Anous stolidus*): on the *qui vive*, head swivelled 180°. vii. American Oystercatcher (*Haematopus palliatus*): a wader heraldically poised to take off. viii. Scarlet Tanager (*Piranga olivacea*): resplendent songbird.

Lavish beyond belief, Audubon's *The Birds of America*, the world's most expensive book (a complete first edition sold for $7.9 million at Christie's, New York, in January 2012) and one of the best-known natural history books ever produced, was first published in double elephant folio size between 1827 and 1839.

Its creator John Audubon led a highly adventurous transatlantic life with more than its fair share of ups and downs. A self-fashioned man, who supported himself by giving drawing classes and doing charcoal portraits for $5, he loved to ramble around the American countryside, executing life size paintings in pastel and watercolour:

> "Audubon was only marginally literate and was indifferent to the truth; he was vain and vulgar, infatuated with the carefully nurtured image of himself as the exotic woodsman, the artist-naturalist with a French accent in flowing ringlets and leather frontier clothes."[1]

Nevertheless he was a pioneer of bird-banding, returning year after year to check on the nesting sites of the Eastern Phoebe (*Sayornis phoebe*), and showed himself to be an astute businessman, employing an assembly line of over fifty aquatint colourists to finish the first edition. The original prints were presented loose leaf in a homespun deal or tin box.

The Natural History Museum, South Kensington, London, has proudly included a *Birds* in its new Treasures Gallery, which features 22 artefacts: the crown jewels of its vast holdings.

1 John Chancellor, *Audubon: A Biography* (London: Weidenfeld & Nicholson, 1978), p.12.

Breathe

Michael Tompert (& Paul Fairchild), 2010
—shot Macbook

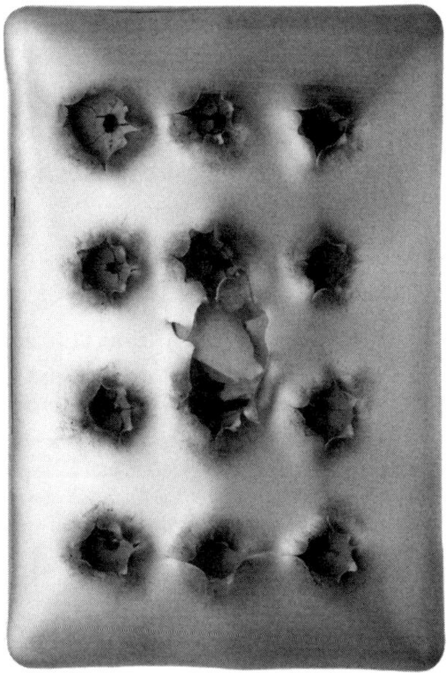

Art and Artists magazine for August 1966 has a striking front cover image of the slashed canvas of a painting by Diego Velásquez, commonly known as the *Rokeby Venus*, 1647–51. The attack was carried out in 1914 by militant suffragette Mary Richardson at the National Gallery, London. Using a meat cleaver she damaged this symbol of female beauty as a protest against the imprisonment of Emmeline Pankhurst, an act described in *A & A* as

> "...possibly the first Auto-Destructive gesture in 19th-century art".

The pace and prolificity of destruction in art most certainly picked up after the Second World War, and went into overdrive during the 1960s. Gustav Metzger's manifestos and his acid/nylon demonstration of 1961 set the agenda. Indeed attacks on property, or the complete debasement of luxury objects, as in Arman's *White Orchid*, 1963—the controlled explosion of an industrialist's MG sports car—were in danger of becoming a transgressive norm, cliché even. The Destruction in Art Symposium held in London in September 1966 witnessed a gathering of activists from across Europe and beyond, ready to use ritual violence for cathartic purposes. The performance element of this era was as important if not more so than the end product, although there is no escaping the vestigial power of Ralph Ortiz's smashed pianos, the strange scrap metal and horse hair sculptures of the minor Viennese Actionist Adolf Frohner, ZERO member Bernard Aubertin's *art brûlée*,[1] and the contribution of John Latham, who was never shy about using books sacrilegiously, copies of *Punch* or legal textbooks handy solid fuel for his infamous 'skoob' towers.

Tompert and Fairchild's shot MacBook *Breathe* sits inside this canon of wilful destructiveness without any difficulty.[2] After buying his gadgets brand new, Tompert subjects them to the blunt force of sledgehammer, saw, Heckler & Koch handgun, blowtorch and train.[3] In this way he has 'enhanced' iPhones, iPads, iPod Nanos and MacBook Airs. The sorry remains of the late Steve Job's finest are then photographed in high-resolution by Fairchild, who artfully recreates Apple product shots, except featuring these totalled devices that ooze a radiant if grungy charm all their own.

Examples of accelerated entropy, defunct phones or books, they speak a mute language of technological collapse, the perverse detritus of Silicon Valley.

---

1 See my 'Strike a Light' in issue no.13 of the web journal */Seconds* www.slashseconds.com

2 Cognate with *Breathe* is *56 Broken Kindle Screens* (2012) created by Silvio Lorusso and Sebastian Schmieg, a print-on-demand paperback of broken e-ink displays.

3 This action found a bizarre political correlate in the destruction of hard drives and memory chips by means of angle grinders and other tools, carried out by a senior editor and a computer expert in the basement of the *Guardian* newspaper. The aim was to obliterate the encrypted files of wanted contractor Edward Snowden. For more see Henrik Olesen's 'Picture Piece', *Frieze*, no.159, November–December 2013.

Catalogue

Essais De Reconstruction D'objets Ayant Appartenu à Christian Boltanski Entre 1948 et 1954

Christian Boltanski, 1971

—offset[1]

Not unlike charity, inventories begin at home, as with those of Rudolf II detailing exotica appropriated from the New World in his Prague *Kunstkammer* (1607–11), Ole Worm's pioneering catalogue *Museum Wormianum* (1655), or the lists of self-styled 'vellomaniac' Sir Thomas Phillipps, known for his financially ruinous manuscript holdings. By comparison Boltanski's wry little *musée* or 'reconstitution', one of a several such attempts to stretch personal time carried out by him in the early 1970s, is both modest and mute, a list of Fort-Da childhood playthings such as a compass, toy car and pencil-sharpener 'modelled' *en pâte* to remake a fictional past, all the while employing a coolly objective, forensic tone to highlight the fundamental absurdity of collecting (or 'collectorexia')[2], a pursuit drenched in melancholy.

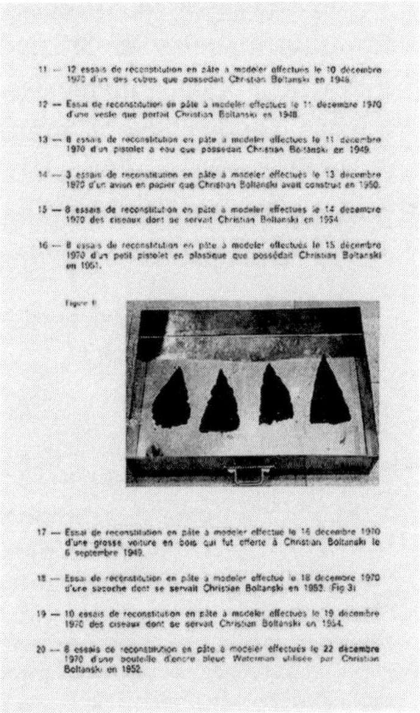

11 — 12 essais de reconstitution en pâte à modeler effectués le 10 décembre 1970 d'un des cubes que possédait Christian Boltanski en 1946.

12 — Essai de reconstitution en pâte à modeler effectué le 11 décembre 1970 d'une veste que portait Christian Boltanski en 1948.

13 — 8 essais de reconstitution en pâte à modeler effectués le 11 décembre 1970 d'un pistolet à eau que possédait Christian Boltanski en 1949.

14 — 3 essais de reconstitution en pâte à modeler effectués le 13 décembre 1970 d'un avion en papier que Christian Boltanski avait construit en 1950.

15 — 8 essais de reconstitution en pâte à modeler effectués le 14 décembre 1970 des ciseaux dont se servait Christian Boltanski en 1954.

16 — 8 essais de reconstitution en pâte à modeler effectués le 15 décembre 1970 d'un petit pistolet en plastique que possédait Christian Boltanski en 1951.

Figure 8

17 — Essai de reconstitution en pâte à modeler effectué le 16 décembre 1970 d'une grosse voiture en bois qui fut offerte à Christian Boltanski le 6 septembre 1949.

18 — Essai de reconstitution en pâte à modeler effectué le 18 décembre 1970 d'une sacoche dont se servait Christian Boltanski en 1952. (Fig 3)

19 — 10 essais de reconstitution en pâte à modeler effectués le 19 décembre 1970 des ciseaux dont se servait Christian Boltanski en 1954.

20 — 8 essais de reconstitution en pâte à modeler effectués le 22 décembre 1970 d'une bouteille d'encre bleue Waterman utilisée par Christian Boltanski en 1952.

More than at any other time in human history, we have surrounded ourselves with objects that confer status and success, the individual a walking endorsement for this age of bloated materialism. That extreme hoarder next door churning their stuff from one room to another is YOU, a consumer disaster waiting to happen. Christian Boltanski and his contemporary Arman were ahead of this curve, the artist/collector almost as important a figure now as the voguish artist/curator, though the compound is not so fashionable and gets less wear. Other *prominente* such as Claes Oldenburg,[3] Sophie Calle and Mark Dion have adopted the kleptic mantle, with its links to the overlapping sense-making discourses of criminalistics and psychoanalysis. The ethnographic turn allows the object to be fetishised, for things do pile up inexorably, accumulated dross almost unnoticed on the tide, the disposable packaging and goods of shopping expeditions with their mad calculus: snap purchases or online click and collect, even foraging trips to car boot and jumble sales. Fatal increments can cause a massive heap at home, proof of failed intimacy starkly exposed in the street, beach or landfill site.

> "He watches the oily water ripple at his feet in a recess of the quay; a few pieces of flotsam have accumulated here: a piece of tar-stained wood, two old corks, a piece of orange peel, and smaller fragments, half-decomposed, difficult to identify."[4]

Unreal estate it could be said, and in Boltanski's case his 'reconstitutions' [5] a struggle to apply an organising principle to things however far-fetched, before they fully possessed him: indexically opaque memories of folly, loss and joy. Little wonder Michael Landy chose to 'granulate' all 7,227 items owned by him during the course of 'Break Down', 2001,[6] and live free of clutter, possibly memory too, a grand yet bathetic gesture generating a coded catalogue to boot, where

> "'A' stood for artworks, 'C' for clothing, 'E' for electrical, 'L' for leisure and so forth."[7]

---

1 Printed to coincide with Boltanski's first solo show at Galerie Sonnabend, Paris, 23 March 1971.

2 Dallas Seitz's, 'Hunted (the cannibalism of colonial collectorexia)', Pump House Gallery, London SW11, 26 October 2007–20 January 2008.

3 In 'Dramaturgy and Gut: Inside Claes Oldenburg's *Mouse Museum*', her review of 'Claes Oldenburg: Mouse Museum/Ray Gun Wing', MOMA, New York, 14 April–5 August 2013, Leora Morinis spots how "The objects seem wilfully tangled between categories. In this way, the installation stays connected—in an intensified form—to certain familiar delights: figurative candy (Coke bottles, Swedish Fish); wearing a stem of cherries as a dangly earring; honey bears. Over time, these things have a tendency to get neutralized, their forms so taken for granted that they slip back into the realm of function. In contrast, the Mouse Museum's objects do not settle down." www.moma.org/explore/inside_out/2013/05/24/dramaturgy-and-gut-inside-claes-oldenburgs-mouse-museum

4 Alain Robbe-Grillet, Richard Howard (trans.), *The Erasers* (London: Alma Classics, 2009), p.16.

5 See Dieter Roelstraete's landmark essay 'The Way of the Shovel: On the Archaeological Imaginary in Art', *e-flux journal* 4, 2009. He makes the case for an 'anarchaeological' role of art, where assemblages of objects do not merely recover what is a ruptured past, but re-write it as in Cypren Gaillard's *Dunepark* (2009) that re-purposed a Nazi bunker.

6 www.artangel.org.uk/projects/2001/break_down

7 Jennifer Mundy, 'Dispossessed', *Lost Art: Missing Artworks of the Twentieth Century* (London: Tate Publishing, 2013), p.240.

Chesil Bank South

Keith Please & Ronald King, 1980
—blind intaglio, letterpress

Differing from its antecedent first edition printed on rag and Glastonbury stock, Please and King's second go at *Chesil Bank South* replaces the old-fashioned geological chart with a blind intaglio version of the Chesilton Bay location, today's Chiswell, and in so doing points decisively beyond the traditional illustrative duplex of lyric poetry and etching, watercolour or silkscreen.[1]

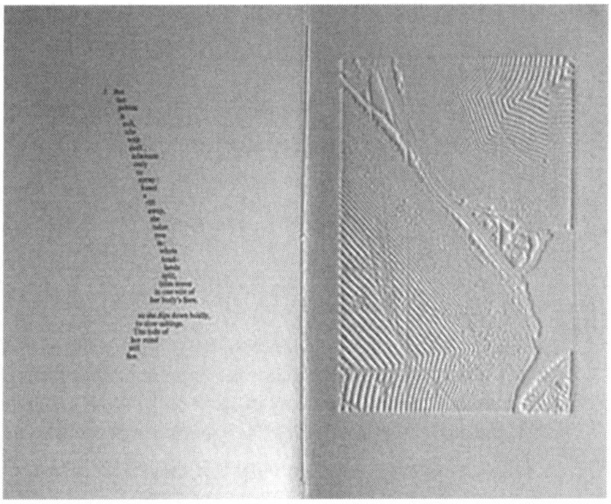

Removing this Circle Press publication from its grey conservation envelope reveals a bleached map that invites you to braille over with an index finger the coastal site as represented, discovering how salient features such as the shoreline or a long since dismantled GWR railway line show up and actually feel. All the legendary signage remains as hollowed out lettering, so the former position of the Coastguard Station, The Mere, and Ancient Landslips can still be determined as embedded naked information, language itself doubling as a type of parlous geographical form, rendering proper names on a material par with contour lines and hatching.

After unfolding Explorer OL15, the 4cm to 1km OS map of Purbeck & South Dorset for comparison, details of the setting on the Isle of Portland really start to show up, as do the changes that have taken place between the era delineated by the original cartography and today,[2] wrought in large part by the ceaseless pummelling of wind and wave against the mainland, which causes the unique durational formation of Dorset chesil, or *ceosel*, the Saxon word for gravel, and thus the unruly harvest of Lyme Bay:

> "June, 1757, a mermaid was thrown up by the sea, between Burton and Swyre, thirteen feet long. The upper part of it had

some resemblance to human form, the lower was like that of a fish; the head was partly like that of a man, and partly like that of a hog."[3]

As the British coastline becomes ever more subject to substantive change,[4] King's cuttlefish-white, subtly tactile map preserves the past and belies David Batchelor's outdated bee-in-the-bonnet thesis that western society is 'chromophobic', colour an object of prejudice. No, *Chesil Bank South* as mapped landscape has more in common with the oil on linen textures of the painter Robert Ryman (for Batchelor an exception proving his dubious rule):

> "Ryman's whites are always just that: whites. His whites are colours; his paintings do not imply or involve the suppression of colour."[5]

---

1 Typified by Richard Bentley's rococo drawings in *Designs by Mr. R. Bentley, for Six Poems by Mr. T. Gray* (1753), often seen as a milestone in book history for its integration of picture and text; so much so that peeved poet Gray insisted on his own name being printed below Bentley's on the title page. The text can be read as e-book at www.ota.ox.ac.uk/id/4609

2 The British Library's new Georeferencer tool allows users to overlay historic maps on top of modern ones. www.bl.uk/maps

3 John Hutchins, *The History and Antiquities of the County of Dorsetshire* (London: Bowyer & Nichols, 1774), p.338.

4 Katrina Palmer's *End Matter* (2015), an Artangel/BBC4 commission, included an audio-visual walk entitled 'The Loss Adjusters', leading from 52 Easton Street, an old loss-adjusters office, past a cemetery to one of Portland's quarries adding a new fictive layer to the peninsula's lode.

5 David Batchelor, *Chromophobia* (London: Reaktion Books, 2000), p.11.

Contraband

Taryn Simon, 2010

—digital photographs, offset

Taryn Simon gave advanced warning of her fascination with smuggled goods in *An American Index of the Hidden and Unfamiliar* (2007–8), which included a trademark high-definition photograph taken in the Contraband Room at John F. Kennedy International Airport, featuring a rotten heap of maggoty fruits and decaying bush meat awaiting dissection and incineration. In *Contraband* she dispenses with captions and gets right down to business, documenting, in 1075 photos, a mountain of objects and packages confiscated by US Customs & Border Protection and the US postal Service both based at JFK, all taken during an intensive intensive five-day residency from 16 to 20 November 2009, in which as Hans Ulrich Obrist duly notes in his introduction (penned at Heathrow Airport):

> "The ideas of the marathon and of the non-place converge."[1]

Alphabetic ironies and strangeness abound. Cheques precede Chicken Feet, Deer Tongues sit next to Diazepam, Jerky juxtaposed with fake Gucci buckles, Stun Guns besides Sugar Cane. Posed and forensically snapped on lunar white backgrounds, these goods float in both a formal and administrative limbo, any narrative significance abruptly foreclosed.

Pirated / Counterfeit / Prohibited / Illegal / Held Pending Appraisal / Undeclared / Accidentally Seized / FAA Violation / Pending Investigation / Unlicensed Dangerous Goods / Incidental To Arrest. These official categories hedge in and fence off US homeland, designed to keep it 'safe' from the the unruly and sinister, holding infection at bay. Pages 246–255 in effect are a mini-gallery: West African voodoo masks with their hidden cargo of wood-boring beetles, Snow White nesting dolls infringing the Disney copyright, anabolic steroids, hallucinogenic Khat (*Catha edulis*), prohibited sausages likewise.

Simon's wholesale prestidigitation renders all this stuff in HD, as close to anonymous as you can get, an entrepôt of miscellaneous objects over which strict legal judgements have been made, variously presented still in their original brown paper packaging, baking foil, Ziplok bags, jam jars, cardboard boxes, cling film, glass phials etc.

> "Most were counterfeit. A photograph is already a copy of something and here I was making copies of copies. I shot them inside jewel-like boxes and they entered another economy—the art market."[2]

Granted, compulsive listing becomes all too easy a way of managing both contents, and the visual shock they deliver. Even the fingernail shadows which these moribund things cast onto their sterile background look as if they could be Photoshopped out, collected. There is a displaced madness here, quotidian yet dreamy, criminally sneaky.

This is a fabulous book, history concealed and congealed in its dry index.

1 See 'Ever Airport: Notes on Taryn Simon's *Contraband*', p.7.

2 'Ready For Your Close-Up?', interview with Sue Stewart, *Evening Standard*, 13 October 2011.

Un Coup de Dés Jamais N'Abolira Le Hasard

Marcel Broodthaers, 1969
—blacklined text, offset

Stéphane Mallarmé's legendary shipwreck poem *Un Coup de Dés Jamais N'Abolira Le Hasard* first appeared in 1897 in the magazine *Cosmopolis*, and was republished in 1914 by the *Nouvelle Revue Française*. It has been described as

> "...an example of a cataclysmic moment in the historical unconscious".[1]

Marcel Broodthaers' cancelled version of the host text owes a formal debt to Man Ray's deleted verse *Untitled Poem, Paris May 1924*,[2] but was also signposted by his own earlier efforts: the pages of *Pense-Bête* (1963–64) were altered by means of tipped-in coloured paper rectangles that thwarted easy reading, while his appropriation of Alexander Dumas's *Vingt Ans Après* (1969), reprinted in its original Livre de Poche format but wrapped in a fluorescent band bearing the name of Broodthaers and R. Lucas, director of the New Smith Gallery, were try-outs for access denial.

These gestures must be seen too in the historical context of 19th century Belgian publishing piracy, which before 1852 brazenly ignored French authors' rights. And yet publishing the 1914 edition of *Un Coup* with its new subtitle *Image* was far more than a fresh outbreak of neighbourly petulance, but a homage in some respects, as Broodthaers stuck to the original press run. Nevertheless his wholesale deletion of Mallarmé's thirty-two page neo-baroque spatial poem attacked the reification of meaning head on, for as Benjamin Buchloh has commented:

> "The double inversion of Broodthaers' 'writing' was that, on the one hand, it seems to engage in precisely that modernist strategy of hermetic resistance by which the visual or linguistic sign constitutes itself to refuse the visual or sensual data which the viewer demands, this refusal operating in the semantic disguise of the construction of an anomic object."[3]

Used as the basis for a group show 'The Space of Words' (Dominique Petitgand contributed *Le Bout de la Langage*, a sound work in which Pinter-like blanks brim full of hypothetical meaning, punctuated snippets of conversation),[4] *Un Coup* is a black op as intrinsically brave as Robert Rauschenberg's *Erased de Kooning Drawing*, 1953, annexing negative space as does the International Necronautical Society today.

Broodthaers conjures a lexical challenge, the common reader's eye and brain forced to admit defeat when faced with the instrumentality of language *sous-râture*.[5]

---

1 Graham Robb, *Unlocking Mallarmé* (New Haven, CT/London: Yale University Press, 1996), p.195.

2 See Francis Picabia's dadaist magazine *391*, no.3, 17 June 1924.

3 Benjamin H. D. Buchloh (ed.), 'Open Letters, Industrial Poems', *Broodthaers: Writings, Interviews, Photographs* (Cambridge, MA/London: MIT Press, 1988), p.73.

4 Musée d'Art Moderne, Grand-Duc Jean, Luxembourg, 19 Febuary–25 May 2009.

5 Vietnamese born artist Albert Dupont addressed the difficulties of reading Mallarmé's original poem by printing it onto six double sheets of transparent polyester which could be overlaid with his own coloured serigraph *Poem-Bloc* (1999), kept in a protective wooden box equipped with five plastic dice.

De Humani Corporis Fabrica Librorum Epitome

Andreas Vesalius, 1543
—woodcut, flap anatomies, letterpress

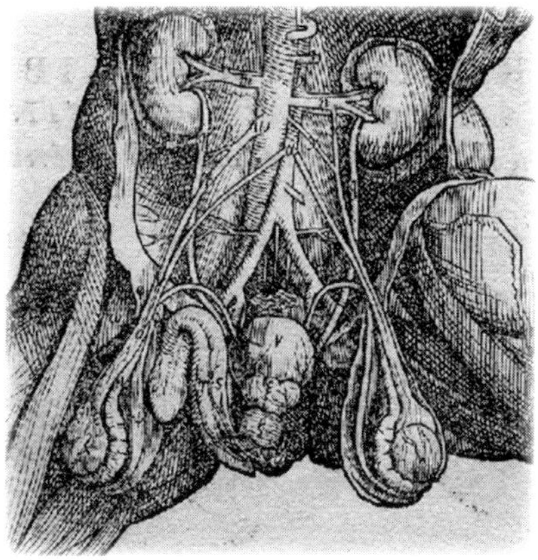

Appearing in 1543, the same year as Copernicus's new celestial model *De Revolutionibus Orbium Colelestium*, Vesalius's *Fabrica* provided a few visceral shocks to match, its implicit interactivity[1] encouraging the reader/user to construct their own anatomised body in a precocious move worthy of Taschen, Dover Publications or Ilex's DIY range over four hundred years later.

The exhibition 'Spectacular Bodies', 2000–2001,[2] gave vent to the manifold secrets of the human body, noting in its catalogue how the illustrated title page of the *Fabrica*

> "...shows the master-dissector performing in his famous hands-on role. The image of Vesalius dissecting at Padua is designed to make a series of polemical points, above all about the primacy of direct experience of human rather than animal bodies. The real body is to become the 'book' to be read by the surgeon rather than the set text sanctioned by traditional learning."[3]

Jonathan Sawday's virtuoso exegesis of this same complex woodcut in the *Fabrica* focuses on the mythological tale of Perseus the hunter, who equipped with sword and mirror overcomes and decapitates the Medusa, becoming for Sawday an emblem of *Anatomia*, the dark side of early modern science:

> "The surgeon seems to share the iconic status of the artist (or the visionary) within our culture, since both are held to be in possession of a privileged gaze which is able to pass beyond common experience, through surface structures, to encounter a reserved core of reality."[4]

In our own time Dr Gunther von Hagens' lurid 'Body Worlds' exhibitions of plastinated corpses have generated many tabloid column inches indicating that to peel back the skin is to reveal we are all 'alike', both gruesome and startling. Similarly Damien Hirst's 20-metre flayed statue *Verity*, 2012, on the seafront at Ilfracombe, Devon, with her exposed pregnant womb and navel ring, divides opinion, blogposts branding it an 'advert', and 'a blot on the landscape'. Jason Freeny's contemporary *demi écorché* figurines of Barbie or Mickey Mouse are also a reminder that this fascination with interiors runs deep, which is why the remarkable set of drawings produced for the *Fabrica* by Dutchman Jan Stephen van Calcar must be seen as epitomising the very search for knowledge itself.

---

1 In their exhibition notes to 'From Woodcut to Photograph: Techniques of Book Illustration', Maughan Library, King's College, London, January–15 April 2014, curators Stephanie Breen and Katie Sambrook observe of the *Fabrica* that "Letters of the alphabet, small enough to label individual body parts without distorting their depiction, act as a key to each illustration".

2 Hayward Gallery, London, 19 October 2000–14 January 2001.

3 Martin Kemp & Marina Wallace, *Spectacular Bodies: The Art and Science of the Human Body from Leonardo to Now* (London/Berkeley, CA: Hayward Gallery Publishing & University of California Press, 2000), p.23.

4 Jonathan Sawday, *The Body Emblazoned: Dissection and the Human Body in Renaissance Culture*, (London/New York: Routledge, 1995), p.12.

Ephemera

Leigh Ledare, 2012

—revues, offset [1]

As curators Alex Kitnick and Andrew Roth's ICA exhibition notes explain:

> "Lee Ledare's *Ephemera* spans six oversize staple-bound fascicles, methodically documenting the slow unveiling of a stack of printed matter. In a clever conceit, Ledare photographs the sheaf on a copy stand from above, removing one sheet from the stack for each new photograph; as each page of the physical book turns, a new printed page appears, the reader's hand mimicking the hand of the artist at work."[2]

At the core of this slick and teasing performativity is Ledare's act of removing pages from vintage publications such as *Time Life*, these tear sheets being supplemented by intimate shots of his near family, thereby blending public and private realms. The note continues:

> "Ledare's compositions operate on two perpendicular planes: the torn sheets placed opposite one another often resonate through visual associations, while each individual page on the stack is framed by the edges of larger ones below, providing anticipatory glimpses of what is to come."[3]

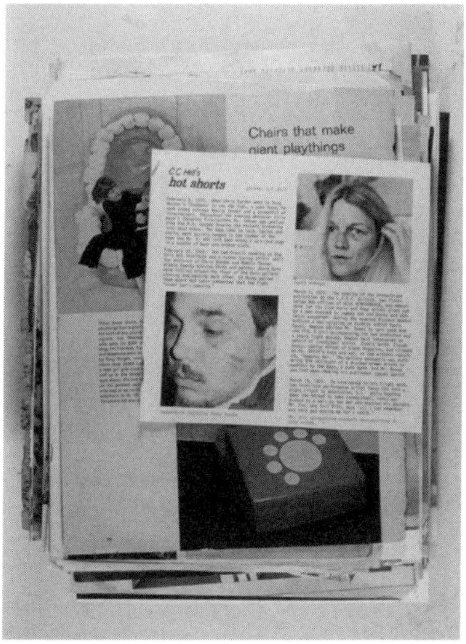

As a photographer, Ledare has gained renown for his louche images, often involving himself or others frolicking on a bed, with suggestions of incest never far away; questioning the shifting nature of human agency and the ethical constraints that hem it in. Through its formal means, *Ephemera* explores informational promiscuity too: the way news stories or feature articles are juxtaposed with glossy advertising, how dreams and desires are conveyed by commercially driven systems of representation that attract yet repel us, personalised yet alien. Those dentist's waiting-room magazines, ads and slogans so full of allure and promise which *Ephemera* treats as a visual bank are fragile, embrittled vehicles of the near past which, when subjected to Ledare's gaze and conceptual apparatus, figure in a novel reading experience, digital publishing swift to remediate, upcycle and remake this apparently faded, forlorn material.

Ephemera showcases Ledare's trash amateur aesthetic and concludes cleverly with a page that discloses the artifice invariably at work in his complex 'real life' scenes:

> "Finally, working entirely through the pile, the back cover of magazine No.6 stands simply as an image of the surface of the copy stand."[4]

---

1 Volume 3 of *Double Bind*, published by MFC-Michèle Didier, Paris.

2 'Paperwork: A Brief History of Artists' Scrapbooks', ICA, London, 1 April–11 May 2014.

3 Ibid.

4 'An Interview' with David Joselit in Elena Filipovic (ed.), *Leigh Ledare, et al* (Milan/Brussels: Mousse Publishing & Wiels Contemporary Art Centre, 2012), p.123.

Fake Hornbook

George Offor?, 1835
—oak mounted text, laminated bone

In appearance hornbooks or 'abseys' were early modern pedagogic aids for children, resembling small wooden bats or racquets (also called 'battledores'), designed either to hang around the neck or from a girdle, so that juvenile learning might be continuous and unavoidable. Generally speaking they bore the ABC, numbers, and the Lord's Prayer, data that would be covered by a thin sheet of translucent horn often kept in place by a metal latten and nails.

In 1845, the pious book dealer George Offor had presented a hornbook to the British Museum, perhaps as a 'spuriosity', a dark provenance hinted at in its catalogue entry

> "A fabrication in imitation of the black letter of the typical orthography employed in the first half of the sixteenth century."

Offor, a polemical Baptist, bibliographer and avid book collector of Grove House, Hackney, is best known today if at all as the editor of the three-volume collected works of John Bunyan, published in 1854.

After his death, Offor's own library was due to be sold by Sotheby's in the Strand during June 1865. Unfortunately, however, the projected eleven day sale of nearly four thousand items was catastrophically interrupted by a fire that destroyed a large part of the stock. Manuscripts, Bibles, psalters, and collections of sermons went up in smoke, as did rare Bunyaniana, such as

> "Lot 2020: An iron pen-case, made by Bunyan, the brazier, with some stumps of old pens. Apple scoop."

The fate of another relic singular for its lack of descriptive rubric in the Sotheby's catalogue, is uncertain:[1]

> "Lot 2024: A hornbook."

An opportunistic dealer, though, William Stevens of St Martin's Lane did salvage several sacks of charred remains from the ruined auction house.[2]

Now well and truly defunct, and classed somewhat snootily along with emblems, chapbooks, zodiacs, quaint board games, playing cards, nosegays, weather vanes, pub signs, canal boat art and wrought-iron work as types of 'folk art', battledores deserve to be re-evaluated as manifest examples of an emergent reading technology, mobile interfaces in effect, their colportage enabling the acquisition of both grammar and calculus.

---

1 It is said Lots 1505–2021 were destroyed, meaning this particular horn book may have been among the holdings rescued and disposed of in the following year by Messrs Pultick and Simpson.

2 "When Sir Leicester Harmsworth's fine Bunyan library came under the hammer in 1946 there appeared in the sale room many charred fragments salvaged from the earlier collection, a melancholy reminder of the disaster." A. N. L. Munby, *The Formation of the Phillipps Library from 1841 to 1872* (Cambridge: The University Press, 1956), p.137.

Firenze

John Latham, 1967
— *books, foam, pipes, tubes*

Strictly speaking a Procrustean relic, *Firenze*[1] was generated in the heat of performance, or performances rather, over the course of four evenings in April 1967 by John Latham and others in the basement of Better Books, Charing Cross Road, London WC2. 'Book Plumbing' consisted of serial happenings: 'Installation', 'Steam Situation', 'Smoke and Plaster' and 'Wind Foam and Dream' performed and projected by Latham, Jeffrey Shaw, Jeffrey Sawtell, Paul Davies, Bob Cobbing and Ernst Jandl (pre-recorded tape).

> "All surfaces, most objects and some people in the basement were covered with newsprint; books were variously destroyed by melting lard, circular saw, setting in gelatine; people and books were connected by pipes and tubing, and encased with polyurethane foam and plaster."[2]

Firenze remains from this visceral spillage of English zaniness, intermediated, a *tafelbuch* and ugly piece of 'documentation', as if illicit salvage from the book hypocausts of Francois Truffaut's film version of Ray Bradbury's dystopian novel *Farenheit 451*, released in 1966. The work's hybrid form perfectly expresses Latham's malignant disregard for the sanctity of books, a portent of the discontinuation of his ILEA contract at St Martin's School of Art in 1968, allegedly for masticating (along with Barry Flanagan) the pages of a library book: Clement Greenberg's collection of critical essays *Art and Culture* (1961).[3]

But it would be wrong to be excessively offended by Latham's utter abuse of books, which could be clean and conceptual as in *Table with the Law*, 1988, or palpably virtuoso as in the hanging plastered orb *Cluster No.11*, 1992. In truth, the ideological systems of Religion, Science and Art History were his real targets (positing their convergence at so-called 'flat time'), and using the bound codex as raw material, a gross, interrogative way for Latham to challenge their entrenched institutional hegemony, purveying his own set of counter-beliefs: a cosmically charged transdisciplinarity little understood during his own lifetime.

Latham would evolve into the inventor of 'time-based theory' and engineer the artist as 'incidental person' in Artist Placement Group (1966–79), a controversial project that attempted a pseudo-Trotskyite penetration of industry. His heterogeneous practice often appears to be the result of a struggle to escape the throes of private language, and his mutant book works crude signals of historical 'closure' or a superseding of the technological epoch facilitated by the Mainz printer Johannes Gutenberg's use of movable type; sinister chronicles of fragmentation, entropy and social malaise.

1 See my review, 'John Latham: 'Distress of a Dictionary'', Flat Time House, London, *Art Monthly*, no.322, December 2008–January 2009.

2 Elisa Kay, Silvia Sgualdini & Mike Sperlinger (eds.), *John Latham Films: 1960–1971* (London: Lisson Gallery & LUX, 2010), DVD booklet, p.39.

3 Stewart Home's blogpost 'Bohemian Blues: John Latham, the birth of Conceptual Art & the 1960s drug culture at St Martin's School of Art' provides a fascinating if cynical take on this episode, going so far as to suggest that the flask containing the original chewed up Greenberg remains *Still and Chew*, 1966–67, may have been adulterated with pages from a Mickey Spillane thriller! See www.stewarthomesociety.org/art/latham.htm

The First of April

A blank Poem, in Commendation of the Suppos'd Author of a Poem Lately Publish'd, Call'd, Ridotto, or, Downfall of Masquerades

The Free Agent, 1724

—letterpress

During that brief informational lacuna as you wait for a webpage to resolve, the words 'about: blank' appear in the browsing tab, along with a placeholder symbol of a foolscap sheet with its top right-hand corner turned down. Blankness, though, is more than a temporary *lorem ipsum* for it possesses an allure, nothingness never a void but the plenary in disguise.[1]

Far from a mere waggish curio, *The First of April*, published by one J. Graves, next White's Chocolate House, St James's Street, is without doubt atypical, and extrudes from its 18th-century literary surroundings, in a manner not unlike *Tristram Shandy*:

> "It's a conceptual poem that exploits its medium, but doesn't it seem[s], rise to the level of a 'poetics of blankness'."[2]

Devised by someone known as The Free Agent, a handle that sounds surprisingly modern, the longwinded title implies that the contents might be a type of Oulipean joke, but its credentials are such that it must be seen as prototypical, belonging to a class of contemporary conceptual 'writing' purveyed by Paul Fournel, Kenneth Goldsmith, Derek Beaulieu, Carolyn Thompson[3] et al.

After a brief dedication To No Body, pages 9–11 contain stranded symbols that draw the bemused reader's eye to correlated footnotes; starry, daggered footnotes without a text! What are we to make of this whimsy?

> "From the Decorations of Ivy, I compare the Brows of an ancient Poet to a window at Christmass."

Such cryptic clues not only highlight the absence of a master poem (*a priori* their very reason for existence), and thus be possible starting points to reverse-engineer a sham Augustan lyric, but also the materiality of the book's feint whiff of snuff.

Modern acts of literary kenosis include Nick Thurston's *Reading the Remove of Literature* (2006), the textual remains of his study notes to Maurice Blanchot's *L'Espace Littéraire* (1955),[4] a project which was then itself subject to further erasure in Kristen Mueller's freebooting rendition *Partially Removing the Remove of Literature* (2014), that opted to save nothing but Thurston's non-verbal diagrammatic traces: arrows, asterisks, brackets along with running titles such as Hölderlin's Itinerary. In the sphere of visual art, Klara Lidén's poster painting sequence involved her appropriation of cruddy chunks of fly-posted matter over which she then stuck low-grade unused paper, a decisive cancellation, making nude screens onto which the public were welcome to project their own visualisations.

1 See Information as Material's digest on nothingness at www.eclipisearchive.org/NOTHING.pdf

2 blog.whitneyannetrettien.com/2010/08/blank-poem-1723-or-present-of-absence.html

3 See in particular her series of drawings 'Gasping for Breath', 2012–2013.

4 www.scribd.com/doc/64261524

Grandes Heures de Rohan

Anon, 1430–1435
—illuminated prayer book

Although in style and content far removed from modern studio practice, much of the show-stopping Gothic handiwork of the Rohan Master, probably in the service of the Anjou dynasty, was carried out under close supervision by a team of nameless assistants.

An illustrative maverick and entrepreneur who arrived in Paris via Provence and Troyes, his workshop broke with the naturalistic line that was the stock-in-trade of the anonymous Boucicaut Master and the three Limbourg brothers, choosing to focus on the human profile rather than form; thereby becoming as a consequence the greatest expressionist in 15th century France. His full page Last Judgement or Lamentation of the Virgin is unflinching depictions of agony. In the latter there is little concern for perspective: the distraught Virgin collapses in the arms of St John, as if a bereaved mother in Gaza caught in the full glare of 24/7 news media, an unforgettable blood-spattered *hoc est corpus* that borders on emotional pornography.

Clearly this artist had absorbed the style and format of the breviary *Les Très Riches Heures* (1412–89), and Angevin bible, basing his pages on the miniature iconography of these lavish books, but went beyond mere derivation, using warping and disproportion to emphasise the everyday human dramas of the Calendar, or grander ones of The Fifteen Petitions to Our Lord and The Office of the Dead. His religious scenes painted on vellum were typically framed inside a main oblong window, which the Rohan Master often elongated, and a moralising side panel that uniquely was given a caption in old French, such tabloidesque compositions, with their use of egg tempera and gold, laid down against the loveliest of botanical wallpapers. So whilst earlier templates of the book of hours were subtly referenced, it was the degree of synthetic variation or recombinance that gave his work its luxurious if gruesome edge; both familiar yet different.

Perhaps, though, it is in his graphic demonology that the Rohan Master comes across at his most Boschian: trademark allegorical figures part of a tradition kept alive today in the curious gridded hieroglyphs of Grisha Bruskin, specifically *Notes Revised 6*, 1995, warnings to remain vigilant to evil impulses during the strictly subdivided canonical hours of the medieval liturgical day.

Halton

Bedford Lemere & Co., 1892
—albumen prints

Included in Sims Reed Rare Books' catalogue *A Selection of Rare Books* (2011), the dealer's description cannot be improved upon:

> "...25 mounted albumen prints on the photographer's original gilt-edged mounts, each with hand written caption in black ink and photographer's gilt stamped credit to lower left. (255 x 305mm). Original blue crushed Morocco wool-lined presentation box, gilt title: 'Halton 1892' stamped to upper board within elaborate gilt tooled decorative borders. £4,500."

Twenty-five Views of Alfred de Rothschild's Halton House, to give it the full title, showcases both this fantastical chateau built by William Cubitt, and the extraordinary photographic prowess of the Bedford Lemere Company, right at the top of its game. A visual record of the private banker's bolt-hole in the Home Counties, this album conveys the shameless opulence of *le style Rothschild*.

Room after room is dressed and padded with lashings of ormolu, gilding, brocade, silk, floral carpets, club furniture, Raj trophies, elaborate urns, vases, and indoor plants. To call it *étouffant* is no exaggeration. Little wonder these prints reveal domestic spaces purged of the human form (a billiard cue left on the baize almost the only trace of recent activity) to offset the lascivious overloaded grandeur, standard at Halton. Every speck of dust and guinea cigar ash has been hounded from sight, every curtain, carpet and drapery absolute in its pristine, uncreased purity. Who could ever have breathed easy in such a choking ambience?

The epitome of a high Victorian show home/mausoleum, and the built equivalent of the Titanic, Halton House was hardly ever used (although the paternalistic Rothschild did build a reading-room stocked with newspapers and journals for local villagers), and the whole Rothschild estate was eventually purchased for the knockdown sum of £112,000 by the government at the end of the Great War, who promptly turned Halton House into an RAF officers mess.

Based in a studio at 147 Strand, London, from 1867 to 1947, Bedford Lemere & Co. were truly renowned architectural photographers with a profitable sideline in cruise ship interiors. Today, over a quarter of their total output of 100,000 images is looked after by English Heritage, including 21,800 glass plates. Other images can be found at the National Maritime Museum, the V&A, the Royal Commission on the Ancient and Historical Monuments of Scotland and RIBA.

Harmonies

Ferrar family, 1625–35
—collage

It was a pleasure to come across an example of the mutilated 17th-century source material[1] used to make a series of fifteen biblical 'harmonies' produced at atelier Ferrar in the hamlet of Little Gidding, Huntingdonshire, England, displayed in one of the themed rooms at Tate Britain constituting the exhibition 'Art Under Attack: Histories of British Iconoclasm' (2013). These evangelical digests were produced by the extended Ferrar family in a special Concordance Room, where Nicholas Ferrar devised

> "...how they should cut out such and such particular passages out of the two printed copies of any part of each Evangelist, and then lay them together so as to perfect such a head or chapter as he designed".[2]

The handiwork was so good that

> "...many curious persons who saw the work when it was done, were deceived, and thought that it had been printed in the ordinary way".[3]

So stationed at cutting desks, Ferrar's daughters and nieces, edified by black letter *sententiae* and mottoes either hung or written in candle soot on the walls of their green room, merged the early modern practice of commonplacing with classical trompe l'oeilism.

Until quite recently, writing on or cutting up books has been frowned upon and even punished,[4] but as Juliet Fleming has pointed out, Ferrar's nieces Anna and Mary Collett would have

"...cut their books... in ways that were free of the modern inhibitions that make such a thing seem scandalous to us".[5]

The 'pasting-printing' technique took place on a risky cusp between bibliographic destruction and the creation of embellished, re-formatted pages that resemble galley proofs, and allowed for non-linear, easy reading comparisons to be made between the varying biblical accounts of Christ's life and death,[6] demonstrating too that the supremacy of the printed word in Europe had still not been fully established by the 1630s; the unbound book a site rather than a surface, being

"...a register of piety".[7]

Clearly where the disciplines of manuscript culture were still alive, a dynamic exchange could take place between these two overlapping material systems, the trimming and collage of the busy Ferrar clan representing a final burst of devotional activity before the execution of Charles I.

---

1 Ferrar travelled extensively on the continent, and acquired many books and Catholic prints. The latter would have constituted his stock, to be used in the production of Little Gidding 'harmonies'. In Tate Britain's 'Art Under Attack', an engraving of *The Last Judgement After Maerten de Vos, c.*1580, was displayed minus two recumbent sheep.

2 Peter Peckard, *Memoirs of the Life of Mr. Nicholas Ferrar* (Cambridge: Cambridge University, 1790), p.204.

3 Ibid., p.204.

4 Take the notorious case of the playwright Joe Orton and his partner Kenneth Halliwell, who in 1962 were each sentenced to "six months gravity" at Her Majesty's pleasure, for the crime of defacing books borrowed from Islington libraries (on release they were additionally fined £262 in damages). In fact the two pranksters were only spicing up many dull texts, and enhancing dust jackets, a genteel if libidinous pastime known as 'extra-illustration' or 'Grangerism' to early 19th century readers.

5 Juliet Fleming, 'Afterword', *Huntingdon Library Quarterly*, no.73, 2010, p.550.

6 U. S. President Thomas Jefferson was a confirmed *découpeur* of Bibles.

7 Adam Smyth, 'Shreds of Holiness: George Herbert, Little Gidding, and Cutting Up Texts in Early Modern England', *English Literary Renaissance*, vol.42, no.3, 2012, p.468.

He Who Sleeps Dines

London Fieldworks, 2011
—record cards, photographs

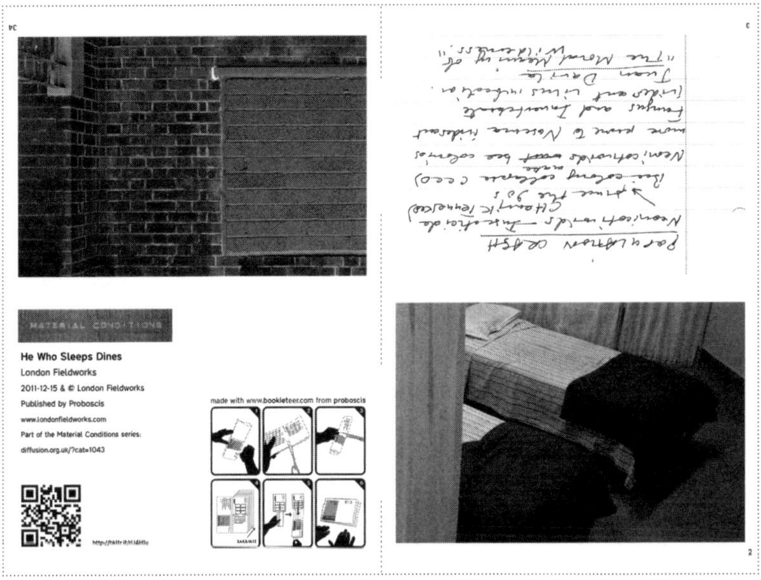

Doubtlessly energy saving, the subject matter of *He Who Sleeps Dines* will appeal to hordes of zonked-out contemporary art practitioners for its espousal of inertia, seasonal hibernation, wildcat striking even, as a metabolic way to re-set their work/life balance. In existence since 2000, London Fieldworks, aka Bruce Gilchrist and Joel Joelson, have collaboratively investigated an array of forms and formats from biorama, space travel, show homes for woodland creatures, outdoor Regency furniture with a twist, video especially devised for mobile caravans, anti-sculpture via EEG readings translated by an industrial robot, and research projects exploring remote and therefore fragile habitats. These strategies situate their zone of operation at the complex interface of cutting-edge technology, nature and human society.

The image sequence of *He Who Sleeps Dines* peddles discourse as story: a neatly folded bed becomes rumpled (London Fieldworks want domestic space to double as a lab for metacognitive research), a young scientist is slumped at his desk (a cautionary tale of self-medication), photoshopped motor vehicles are protected under tarps (implying shut down, or 'colony collapse'). Molecular diagrams, memos and shopping lists of common pharmaceuticals trail the diminished oxidisation of deep sleep, and of falling back on that most despised quantum, fat!

He Who Sleeps Dines is part of the excellent 'Material Conditions' series of ebooks published by Proboscis all of which can be digested as free downloadable pdfs, assembled as A6 booklets at home,[1] or purchased as a case bound set.[2] Very much required reading for would-be professionals, *He Who Sleeps Dines* is a how-to manual for those artists who find their pockets empty in a time of austerity, socially embedded yet wrestling with questions of personal identity and worth, not unlike the superfluous heroes of so much 19th century Russian literature. That said, it would make sense to read it in conjunction with *Something More Than Just Survival* by Janet Owen Driggs & Jules Rochielle, a polemical text in the same Material Conditions series that consists of a report from Occupy LA, and an account of SPAN or Social Practices Art Network, a positive response to so-called unemployment, that tackles the issue of digital isolation, or what they parse as a loss of 'human communion'.

---

1 "There is a choice of a sadistically concise, six-stage diagram (only helpful if you were good at following Kinder Surprise instructions) or a video set to an annoyingly chirpy soundtrack." Jennifer Thatcher, 'Artists' Books', *Art Monthly*, no.354, March 2012.

2 diffusion.org.uk/?p=2566

A Humument

Tom Phillips, 1970
—mobile app

To mark Tom Phillips' seventy-fifth birthday, 24 May, 2012, Thames & Hudson released the 5th edition of his never-ending magnum opus *A Humument*—its title morphed from W. H. Mallock's neglected Victorian novel *The Human Document* (1892). This incorporates much re-worked material, with more than half the pages of the 1980 edition updated.

> "Each page of Mallock's saggy and sanctimonious triple-decker has been painstakingly doctored, drawn and painted over, leaving isolated clusters or words and phrases."[1]

The inherent possibilities[2] of remixing or 'monstering' a found text were still in their infancy when Phillips set out in 1966 on his treatment of a junk shop novel, whose only selection criteria was that it cost 3d or less. Incredibly Phillips has now developed *A Humument* as an app for iPhone and iPad, which comes with special features to enhance the reader's enjoyment:

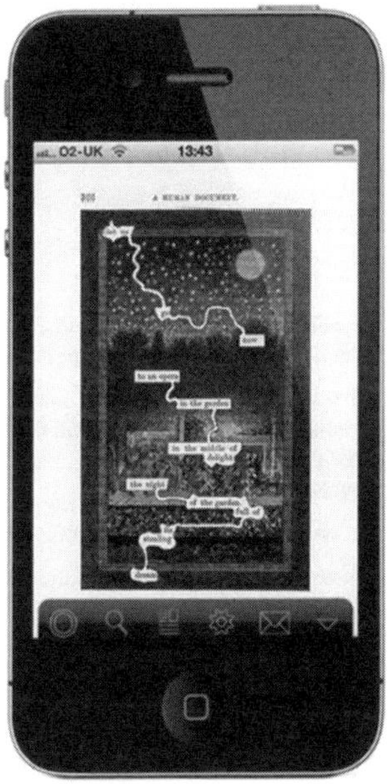

> "The original pages have been rescanned enabling the user to zoom in and view details at higher resolution. The find wheel spins through the book with thumbnail images so you can navigate quickly to your favourites. There are thirty-nine new and previously unpublished pages to discover and an entirely novel interactive feature, the oracle."[3]

However Daniel Traister from the Department of Special Collections, Van Pelt-Dietrich Library, University of Pennsylvania, notes how the scrapbook protocols were already dormant inside Mallock's introduction, and has some surprisingly begrudging things to say about *A Humument*:

"Underlying the apparent stability of Mallock's novel, and of the late Victorian period generally, is an undertone of instability."[4]

Reading between the lines, Traister seems to be accusing Tom Phillips of dilettantism, and running an autocratic statelet, the end product a result of cosmetic surgery rather than deep transformation; but this is a debatable viewpoint, for Phillips has succeeded in producing that most Renaissance of forms, a micrososmos, while 'treatment' implies curing or eradicating a disease, the chronic symptoms of which present in *A Humument* as undertext.

The madeover album pages with their intestinal speech bubbles of aphoristic fragments are designed to be viewed as 'hangs' in pictorial space, troubling memoranda of the bound book's material substrate rather than read systematically. Phillips' pop repertoire of cloisonné stars, swirls and blotches, South London *sfumato* and Klee-like lines washes with aplomb over every trace of the Victorian original's poet manqué, Robert Grenville, who is replaced by the altogether more salacious if metatextual 'Bill Toge', for as Gill Partington has wryly observed *A Humument* is

"...one long and colourful Freudian slip, allowing Mallock's buttoned-up novel to say what's really on its mind."[5]

1 Gill Partington, 'Never Mind the Mallocks: Missing Text in Tom Phillips's *A Humument*', *Critical Enquiry*, vol.55, no.4, December 2013, p.67.

2 Gary Goldstein's *Lotto: An Altered Book* (1994) is a notable recent example of the remastered book. Its hybridity comes from Goldstein's repertoire of inky deletion, Keith Haring-like symbols such as riveted body parts, chimneys, insects and Secessionist lettering borders that combine to evoke the Holocaust.

3 www.tomphillips.co.uk/studio-blog/item/5176-a-humument-app

4 www.tomphillips.co.uk/humument/essays/item/5865-w-h-mallock-and-a-human-document-by-daniel-traister

5 Partington, *op. cit.*, p.68.

Kubla Can't

Tony Kemplen, 1996
—tracing paper, toy letterpress

Tony Kemplen's's[1] introductory spiel about the making of *Kubla Can't* has the authentic tone of the back street anarchist ventilating a how-to description of his seditious methodology (as if he had just discovered printing and quickly decided to throw a spanner in the works), while probably being aware that the chances of it ever being replicated were slim, next to zero in fact.

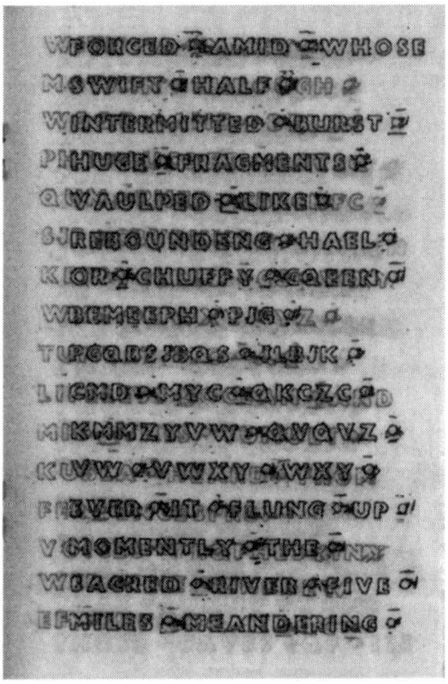

> "Kubla Can't has been typeset using the font that comes with the 'Petite Mini Printer'. This toy printing press consists of a set of moveable type in bright yellow plastic which is then set in a red plastic chase. The finished text is printed by running it through a toy printing press, the pressure being used to transfer ink from carbon paper onto the printing stock."

The name of Kemplen's imprint, Ring Pull Press is suggestively chummy too, implying that all you need do is take a swig of Skol or McEwan's Export, then just get on with it (i.e. desecrating Coleridge's opiated masterpiece); the delinquent *echt* taste of Sheffield 1996.

> "The font supplied, which is about 30 point size, has a limited number of characters or 'sorts', so that as each sort runs out a substitute letter is used. At first words remain recognisable, but soon, as the font gets more and more out of sorts, the only vestige of the original word is its length. When all the letters are used up the type is distributed back into its case and the whole process started again. For this poem the font is used up 10 times."

Evidently influenced during his formative years by a visit from Ronald King[2] of Circle Press fame to Sheffield Hallam University, where he was engaged in a printmaking degree, Kemplen's Mad Hatter cookbook discourse still hasn't finished though:

> "To make the book, rubbings were taken of the type in its chase and reduced to one third actual size. The mirror image produced by this technique is retained by printing onto tracing paper, allowing the text to be read through the page. In this way, the upside down, back to front world of the typesetter is preserved in the book, though in this case, unlike Coleridge's Xanadu, opium played no part!"

So there you have it, a laborious process delivering strings of often meaningless capitalised letters, junk genes that serve no apparent purpose, formatted as dyslexic Trajanic inscription, scrambling the original verse:

> HUGE FRAGMENTS VAULPED LIKE REBOUNDING HAEL OR CHUFFY CQEEN BEMEEPH PJG PGQBSJBQS JLBJK CMD MYC QKCZC KMMZYVW QVQVZ VW VWXY EVER IT FLUNG UP MOMENTLY THE SACRED RIVER

---

1 Kemplen's work includes mail art, printed multiples, sound, installation and joiner's photography. His amended found object *Bolshevik Typewriter Fingering Chart* (1995) is noteworthy. He contributed regularly to Jane Pollard & Iain Forsyth's influential object-based magazine *Words & Pictures: Ultra-Paranoid (Extra-Spatial) Portable Art* (1994–97).

2 "What Ron did was to break the rather—to me—ghastly, traditional mould of British private press publishing. There was a certain idea that the text wasn't important as long as it was all very well printed on beautiful paper and beautifully bound, and that the images mustn't be in any vulgar printing technique—for example, they could be etchings or engravings and they could be woodcuts and, if you were really willing to stretch a point you could try a lithograph. But screenprinting? Forget it." Ian Tyson, 'Thirty Years of Circle Press' in Cathy Courtney, *The Looking Book: A Pocket History of Circle Press 1967–96* (1996), p.20.

Lectures Pour Tous

Stéphane Le Mercier, 2010
—offset

Perhaps echoing the title of a popular illustrated French revue *Lectures pour Tous* (1898–1974), Stéphane Le Mercier's A3 catalogue undoes from inside cardboard covers to reveal thumbnail images of the front covers of all the books he acquired from Pierrot, a mysterious Marseilles book dealer, or *bouquiniste*, between 2006 and its publication four years later.

According to Le Mercier, Pierrot was in the habit of displaying his stock in the street using a kitchen table, painted canvas and plastic chair as props. The hieroglyph has a ramshackle surrealist quality. Pierrot's subsequent disappearance makes *Lectures* all the more poignant as a homage.

Le Mercier's concise index of the thirty acquisitions (all bought for one euro or less) reveals his fascination with the ephemeral, and talent for finding artful ways to organise and bring about its fixity.

> "Paradoxalement, ce livre d'artiste est un catalogue stricto sensu. Il désigne un ensemble de signes et de mots dont les qualités combinatoires, l'économie diffuse s'opposent aux formes réifiées de la culture."[1]

A booklet from the same year: *Rare Postcards from Iceland* continues in a similar direction, bluffing the reader from the word go, as the publication itself contains no actual reproductions of tourist postcards, but contents itself with flat sentences such as

> "One of the 115 craters of the infamous Laki Fissure eruption, 1783."

And,

> "The midnight sun. Near Akreyri, northern Iceland."

This history-from-below focus on recording the transitory raises important questions about the curatorial criteria which determine where a collection should begin and end, and what agreed-upon notion of value—be it attached to either the single specimen, diverse range of objects or congeries—shapes a museum's acquisition policy?

Le Mercier is a tongue-in-cheek artist/curator who challenges the idea of a comprehensive collection and plenipotentiary knowledge, a Frenchman NOT under the influence of Flaubert's farcical encyclopaedia *Bouvard et Pécuchet*.[2]

---

1 "Paradoxically, this artists' book is a catalogue in the strict sense, one that designates a set of words and signs whose combined qualities, and whose literal dispersion go against the norm." www.stephane-le-mercier.blogspot.co.uk/2010/06/lectures-pour-tous-publication.html

2 Memorably described by Cyril Connolly as "…the Baedeker of futility", *Enemies of Promise* (London: Penguin Books, 1961), p.54.

Libretto

Nick Crowe & Ian Rawlinson, 2011
—prototype, news media

The dyadic team of Nick Crowe and Ian Rawlinson have been scarifying public space together since 1994. In *Mugger Music*, 1996, a lone participant was solicitously guided through alleyways, car parks and a pool hall while listening to noise on headphones. *Two Dutch Masters*, 2000, involved the pair allegedly consuming illegal substances in a car, while *Explaining Urbanism to Wild Animals*, 2002, struck a Beuysian note minus the Romanticism; Cheshire's trembling fauna alerted to explicit ecological threat by played-back recordings of construction site din at wildlife habitats such as a burrow and pond. Their video *Opera*, 2011, showcased

> "...appropriated content from a US military manual—banal and insidious phrases such as 'drop your weapon or an American soldier will shoot you' or 'please stand back'—and formatted it into an opera. The statements have been translated into various languages, acting as a manual for potential future conflicts. I guess you just never know when you will need to say 'I'm going to put a capture tag on you' in Russian."[1]

Cognate with it, *Libretto* was due for publication in 2012, in the wake of the Abbotabad SEAL raid that saw Osama Bin Laden's summary execution, but today exists purely as a prototype.

> "I'm afraid that project is in limbo—a couple of dummy copies were produced but it never went to full production (publisher ran out of money!) We're thinking at the moment that we might produce it as a short run—maybe 10 copies or so. But at the minute it remains an unpublished work."[2]

Long-since-removed promotional images from the Merkske website showed how the content of *Libretto* tapped into the global zeitgeist: news media conveying a view of the world as a dynamic ideological battleground, a tight fit between image and caption, peddling a mundanity, in the convoluted words of Dave Beech

> "...integral to the objects, products and images that saturate the everyday. Ubiquity is mundane and mundanity is ubiquitous. But more than that, ubiquity has become the dominant quality of mundanity."[3]

In the creative space of their 'double-retort' Crowe & Rawlinson's work bridges the gap between street and gallery, university and 'real life', homeland and no-man's land.

---

1 'You Are the Company in Which You Keep', *Art Monthly*, no.373, Febuary 2014.

2 Nick Crowe (email, 1 November 2014).

3 'Double, Double' in *Nick Crowe & Ian Rawlinson*, Manchester City Galleries, 3 May–15 June, (2003), p.20.

Lindisfarne Gospels

Eadfrith, Ethelwald, Billfrith, Aldred, *c.*700
—pigment, vellum

The *Lindisfarne Gospels*, a Hiberno-Saxon codex made in the *scriptorium* at Lindisfarne around 700 AD, has survived the dissolution of the monasteries and a fire in Sir Robert Cotton's library in 1731. Written in high status uncial script, it is dedicated to St Cuthbert, and to this day some of the book's illuminations remain unfinished, its survival a reminder that

> "...books as objects were important as more than simple verbal records. They might have talismanic potency, especially if associated with a saint or embellished with complex illumination or an elaborate cover. Famous instances, such as the Lindisfarne Gospels, were carefully (often miraculously) preserved through the vicissitudes of the centuries for all those reasons."[1]

Renowned for its highly ornate *incipit* capitals, and so-called 'carpet pages'—decorative panels in the Coptic style that function as psychological prayer mats for the devotee—and canon tables set in arcades, the Lindisfarne text was glossed word for word by Aldred in the 10th century, his interlinear translation into English, the oldest extant version.

But the physical preparation would have been significant too, requiring up to 150 skins of yearling calves, soaked, stretched and scraped clean in order to make the 259 pages of the Gospels.

> "Before writing began, four large sheets of vellum were stacked and folded in half to form a gathering of eight leaves, 16 pages. To make the book, gatherings of four sheets of vellum were sewn onto leather cords, the ends of which were threaded into thick wooden boards and secured with wooden dowels. Then the boards and spine were covered with damp leather."[2]

Orpiment, red lead, verdigris, chalk, egg shell, gold leaf and carbon are just some of the alchemical substances used in the material production of this vibrant text, typified by its intense spiral and knot work, its pinwheels, vortices and bird zoomorphs. Six years in the making amid an offshore environment lashed by fierce Scandinavian winds, its expert handiwork carried out using sharpened goose quills, twelve hundred years later the *Lindisfarne Gospels* would provide a psychological lattice for the Northumbrian poet Basil Bunting, a reference point for his long dialect poem *Briggflatts* (1966).

1 T. A. Heslo 'As she was writ' *TLS* 8 June 2012, reviewing *The Cambridge History of the Book in Britain vol.1 c.400–1100* Richard Gaemson (ed.) (Cambridge University Press, 2012).

2 www.bbc.co.uk/tyne/features/gospels/gospels_monks_at_work.shtml

Exposé

"All we have is the future."

—Isidore Isou, *Traité de Bave et d'Éternité* (1951)

"For an artist to have an aesthetic philosophy is poisonous in this country, you can get shot for that."

—Alan Reynolds, *Daily Telegraph* (4 September 2014)

Prolegomena

Presupposing the artists' book to have essential qualities, and a need to circumscribe the medium, are the two most pronounced tendencies to bedevil the emergent discipline since Germano Celant's groundbreaking exhibition catalogue *Book as Artwork 1960/1972* (1972).[2] By addressing the diverse and sometimes stellar results of these limiting conditions, this survey and speculative thesis will as a matter of necessity attempt to reconceive the artists' book.

It must be duly noted that this acute moment of historical revisionism or theoretical turn comes with its own set of dangers, not the least of which is necro-institutionalisation, for even if *Unshelfmarked* succeeds in breaking down entrenched attitudes, this could only lead to a new if somewhat veiled orthodoxy; a pitfall to be avoided at all costs in staking out a new past, ironically in itself a futurist coup!

Taking as given Anne Mœglin-Delcroix's acute observation[3] that the artists' book owes more to the pamphlet (*opuscule*) than the tome (*opus*): edgy, independent, sometimes clownish or bawdy, and hard-to-fathom (the result of an exciting collision between craft/fine art skills and new possibilities for production, distribution and dissemination), its cellular heritage and reach in a 21st century landscape of collapsed grand narratives has been extended, despite a hard-to-relinquish attachment to an incumbent paper-bound model of publishing, by the interactive, networked platforms of a worldwide digital publishing revolution.

The debate concerning the nature and meaning of the artists' book, and how it might be defined, has been vortical and bottomless for the last forty years, although summarising the different stances and pedagogical positions adopted by the main critical players and proponents is beyond the scope of this argument, and extraneous to it. But figures such as Lynda Morris, Johanna Drucker, Stefan Klima, Lucy Lippard, Clive Phillpot,[4] Joan Lyons, Riva Castleman, Ulises Carrión,[5] Maurizio Nannucci, Anne Mœglin-Delcroix, Guy Bleus, Stephen Bury and Rob Perrée[6] constitute a kind of informal guild. However, *Unshelfmarked*'s main aim is to categorically break free of the discursive formation left by their pioneering work, or what could be termed, in a nod to theoretical physics, the Standard Model.

This theoretical, indeed theatrical Old Testament phase of the artists' book with its rough-hewn demarcations, epiphanies, convictions, dogmas, decrees, libels and prophecies is over and done with, the format quantified; the Snark netted. Now it can be seen how an often quarrelsome recursivity, part and parcel of the polymorphous artists' book becoming a serious discipline after the Second World War, represented the growth of an academic armature necessary to its acceptance as a cultural fact, not to mention market viability.

The positivist canard that William Blake's *The Marriage of Heaven & Hell* is the original artists' book[7] has become received wisdom in a field whose practitioners, curators, professors and sundry spokespersons have sought to legitimise as distinct from other branches of art history. To designate an originary moment is to open an archive, to establish a timeline and thus start to write a history, alpha to omega. Empires have been built on less. But it must be remembered that Celant's formula was 'book as artwork', book *qua* artwork (and vice-versa), suggestive of disguise, of substitution (or 'passing' as the Elizabethans put it), of intrusion, miscegenation, fraud and Kittleresque switching. Such an implied mutability, while signalling that Celant was cautious about opening up a new field (perhaps allotment would be a better metaphor?), and had no idea where he or it was going, has without doubt dogged the artists' book, since most of its practitioners were still subliminally referencing and paying homage to the 'artwork', i.e. painting or sculpture, and so still functioning in the catholic shadow cast by what were then the two principal art school disciplines. Therein lies a promising thought-line.

But slyly extending the canonic scope of the artists' book to include an 18th-century genius as the founding father says much about unconscious motivating factors.[8] Zeroing in on a fraught visionary who received little acclaim in his own lifetime, whose proverbial skills as poet/illustrator constituted a powerful multi-sensory gestalt, reveals how a proto-Romantic template was set in stone both psychologically and formally for the artists' book, one fatally emphasising the sub-genre's alterity. Yet despite this urge to allow the canonic inclusion of a singular work belonging to an era well before the perplexing signifier 'artists' book' became a currency, on its own this impulse to backdate and reclassify was and still is insufficient, pusillanimous even. Why? Because various naïve landmark 'bibliographic' statements with properties and features bearing more than passing resemblance to what would come to be described as an artists' book were made long before in prehistory, and certainly before the birth of the codex; part of an unacknowledged, overlooked, missing lineage albeit expressed in a wide range of media, that stretches across time to our turbulent era. It is this archive showing up on the ground radar which will be exhumed, and reviewed.

In short, the vague qualifier 'artists'' when conjoined with a pedantic employment of the term 'book',[9] or any bound multi-section data-bearing object,[10] created an airless compound that cordoned off the identity of the phenomena at an early stage, causing a type of fairly predictable stultification. In the capitalist west, foreclosure of shock led to a blinkered attitude towards the irreverence and crudity of Russian Futurist books, making it institutionally impossible to disentangle these critical grenades from Marxist discourse and state propaganda, and thereby judge their importance. As a consequence the rarified world of the artists' book has been blinded by its own limited protocols, the very protocols that emerged as a result of the artists' book 'wars' of the 1980s: intellectual sniping characterised by an absurdist obsession, with where exactly to place the greengrocer's apostrophe, a grammatical hiatus the satirical magazine *Private Eye* has neologised as *hochkommakrankheit*.[11]

Bubbles are made to be burst; the authorised version overwritten.

1. *Archaic Marks*

At the human project's literary outset: the Magdalenian tablet, the cave slab, their symbolic freight of stories traded via a gestural vocabulary of chevrons, *bâtonnets*, stitchmarks, ladders, dots and wavy lines: a semi-delirious subterranean record of key events, be they birth, hunting expeditions, marriage, oneiric imagery or death. Several things support such interpretive musing on Dordogne Valley *plaquettes*: their handiness and portability, their characteristic vocabulary of double-sided burin marks, cover graphics in the form of tracks, animal outlines (e.g. wild fowl, bison, auroch, deer) and scorching.

The humans responsible for decorating these mysterious stones are forever anonymous, but microscopic analysis of individual marks has been able to identify up to a certain point unique ballistic traces left by them.

Genuine authorship.

To examine incised Ice Age *plaquettes*: flat or delaminated slabs of limestone, sandstone and slate (even stalagmites and bone shoulder-blades in some instances), but under 20cm across and 4cm thick, is to be struck by their similarity in terms of size to the post-Gutenberg duodecimo book itself. Usually rhomboidal, or broken bits of rhomboids, their dimensions and how they turn up in cave systems, dropped casually or as spoilheaps[12] strongly suggests the intense epistemological heat signature of what we now call a library, dark deposition sites of symbolically significant 'art', and the very first torchlit loci of pinacographic space.[13] Not yet haunted by the presence of other systematised collections, this is a cavage without precise order, its status part of a fractured network of underground archaeology. Dumped in a midden at the outer edge of prehistorical knowledge, these objects are perfect vehicles for the inscription of transitory psychic states, Orphic leftovers of what Gaston Bachelard the great non-Euclidean anti-positivist termed a 'conjugation',[14] the world merged with its dreaming subject.

Regarding usage, the learned jury is still out. Ideas range from a ritualistic hunting function, to doodling, storytelling, votive lamps, paving stones, even bed warmers. NOT to now add artists' book to this interpretative list would be a casual prejudice, especially as Magdalenian *plaquettes* conform to several key indicators of the normative artists' book, i.e. are home-made (unique/multiple), samizdat, heterodox, and involve phantasmatic visual elements. They are lapidary (literally) but without grandiosity; in short fungible book-like thingies, statistical outliers that despite their remoteness as data points, strengthen the new theoretical model being built in *Unshelfmarked*.

Plaquettes, or little plaques, mark obscure time, mark temporally elusive calendrical moments, long before ticking time's discovery, externalisation and hypostasis as anything more than the innate circadian pulse of life, long before its tyrannical inculcation within Newtonian industrial society as the surveilled perimeter wall of inhuman productivity levels, so prior to its absolute quotidian reign enforced via an unrelenting machinery of deadlines, quotas and targets, its latterday stretching and veritable over-writing upon harried digital staff in their cave 'n' commons offices, upon outsourced contractors, and zero-hours service personnel; the remorseless hegemony of a financial dictatorship that never sleeps.

Similarly, the extraordinary cache of Roman leaf-tablets excavated at Vindolanda auxiliary fort, Northumberland from 1973 by archaeologist Robin Birley of over 750 missives, retrofit the profile. Written in an old cursive hand using a carbon-based ink on birch, alder and oak bark they date from AD 92–130 (just before the construction of Hadrian's Wall), and convey messages about both personal and military matters whether a birthday invitation, an account of fighting the ancient Britons, a request for leave, or the need for warm socks: vivid correspondence from a garrison at the outer edge of the Roman Empire.

The leaf-tablets in this preserved hoard are around 8 x 20cm (each come with stab-holes allowing a thong to lace them shut) as if picture postcards. Economy of means plus personalised content gives these fragile pieces of bark a most particular allure, not to mention importance, as evidence of the tough daily life of Roman soldiers. The Vindolanda cards are suspended forever in an administrative in/outbox, a pile of smudgy letters, the circumstance of their discovery not unlike finding a secret stash of 'outsider' writing or exotic illustrations abandoned in an attic.

The *Voynich Manuscript* (*c.*1400s) can be evaluated in these terms too, an unintelligible hotch-potch of esoteric herbal, astronomical, culinary and pharmaceutical symbols and diagrams, a headache written in a coded language that might be Manchu, might be Greek shorthand, might be a verbose letter-based cipher or a treatise on nature in 170,000 glyphs, containing a map with fold-out pages of islands or 'rosettes', with images of wild flowers that are slightly 'off'; and there again might just be plain gibberish, and a hoax to boot; in short a site of contested provenance, author or authors unknown,[15] an incomplete gall ink text that has been bound and rebound so affecting its pagination, a cranky codex that has been retouched and is ultimately a highly unstable tease that has passed through many hands and invited cryptographic research that has seen the manuscript converted onto IBM punch cards. Latterly *Voynich* has become the source for video games such as *Assassin's Creed IV*, and *Broken Sword: The Sleeping Dragon*.

And so these proto artists' books can be slotted without too much difficulty inside the boundaries of the retro-model being constructed here.

2. *Types of Opulence*

The age of religious Fine Art was characterised by ecclesiastical craftsmanship of the highest order, as found in the *Leabhar Cheanannais* (AD *c.*800) with its decorated initials, Celtic knots and zoomorphs, or *The Luttrell Psalter* (*c.*1320–1340), pious manuscripts that literally illuminated reading experience by using tooled gold leaf. Yet despite their learned weight and opulence, these hefty, highly wrought books have never been remotely considered or taxonomised as original artists' books,[16] their production accredited to anonymous or biographically obscure agencies.

Often cheesily called medieval 'best sellers', Books of Hours were manuscripts designed to render a pious focus and temporal structure to the day for rich and well-connected users. Compendia of miscellaneous texts, emblazoned with initials and decorative or armigerous borders, they allow us a look-see into the daily round: workmen chopping down a tree, knights on horseback or lascivious courting couples, their mood often one of momentary suspension and Arcadian serenity. But the primary purpose of Books of Hours was devotional: prayers and psalms to the Virgin Mary, that divided time into Matins, Lauds, Rime, Tierce, Sext, None, Vespers, Compline.

William de Brailes, Simon Bening, Maïtre Francois, Jean Fouquet, Pseudo-Jacquemart and Gerard Horenbrout are just a few verified names responsible for the illustrative payload of European Books of Hours. Borrowing framing devices used for ecclesiastical icons, such as the *cassetta*, *aedicular* surround and full rood screen, they transferred the psychological *mise-en-scène* of worship from church to banqueting hall or bedroom, altering the quality of that experience and empowering users. Bringing conviviality to believers' relationship with the deity means that Books of Hours must be re-considered as cryptic examples of the artists' book, miniature 'apps' even, under the absolute epistemological rule, regime and domestic confines of popish sanctity.

The urge to retrospectively confer artists' book status upon guidebooks such as Thomas Gray's *Country Houses* (1787) with its terminal blanks for stagecoach jottings, William Gilpin's famous topographical *Observations* (1791–1809) with floral gilt borders, decorated spines, and lemon-yellow edges, or the copiously illustrated index *Where Shall We Go?—a guide to the healthiest and most beautiful watering places in the British Islands* (1864) is hard to resist too. A host of specialised and often enchanting bibliographic novelties e.g. myrioramas (painted cards with millions of permutations) and chromolithographed paper roses would slowly emerge too within the context of popular late 18th-century tourist literature, catering for travellers in search of the picturesque to use in the field, or Baedeker travellers on a foreign holiday. *Vade mecum* traits such as limp cloth, bromide photography, aquatint plates, hand-coloured linen maps folded into a pocket, and silk markers would subliminally affect the dynamic morphology of the 20th century artists' book, both in its conceptual structure and user-friendliness; what might speculatively be called the 'Wye Valley Effect'.

So travel literature is part of an extended continuum, an *ars apodemica*, and its most recent manifestations neatly recapitulate the alleged 'descent' from *livre d'artiste* to democratic object as a *fugueur*'s time capsule. Take high-end merchandise such as Peter & Alison Smithson's *AS IN DS: An Eye on the Road* (1983), their account of a middle-class roadtrip, the layered documentation of Richard Long's *Cerne Abbas Walk* (1975),[17] or down the cobbles of Sharon Kivland's feminist navigation *Les Passages Couverts* (1998), and thence onto the superinformation highway itself with Mishka Henner's *No Man's Land* (2011), a curation of Google Street View images of Mediterranean roadside sex workers, Mark Pawson's laserprint and sticker defacement *Everybody's Mapping Now* (2012), while for the knapsacker there is Emma Cocker & Sophie Mellor's *Manual for Marginal Places* (2011) and Nick Papadimitriou's (aka the 'London Perambulator') *Scarp* (2012), which discloses an off-the-beaten-track *prakrti-laya* London, hand woven into the everyday as if an extra-mural cultural geography course; sundry locative media that sees GPS data integrated with digital reading interfaces.

The librarian and historian of the artists' book Stephen Bury has argued that the 18th-century digressive novel *The Life & Opinions of Tristram Shandy, Gentleman* (1759) is NOT an artists' book; however it contains features such as a black page and marbling[18] that challenge this assertion, while the text's non-linear narrative readily ends itself to remix and treatment, tailor-made for hypertextuality. Commissioned by The Arion Press,

John Baldessari's input to an accordion-folded *Shandy* (1988) was a set of 39 photo-collages, many featuring ghostly characters from B-movies, their faces blotted out by geometric shapes, whilst Visual Editions' *Shandy* (2011) includes innovative layouts, with striking red manicules, chapter headings, pagination and erasure.[19]

Late 19th-century Parisian *livres d'artistes*[20] were created at the confluence of the text and the image,[21] many possessing an undeniable dialogical charm. They were mainly commissioned pieces, expensive and bespoke, printed in small runs, with *exemplaires de tête* on special paper or vellum, and housed in lavish boxes. This tradition was established and sustained by several key personalities: Ambrose Vollard, a pioneer who laid down a marker with a limited edition of Paul Verlaine's *Parallèlement* (1900), printed on Dutch weave with the watermark PARALLELEMENT, and erotic lithographs by the post-impressionist painter Pierre Bonnard; Daniel-Henry Kahnweiler an art dealer turned publisher, renowned for doing away with margins, pagination and captions, and the galerist Aimê Maeght, who ran the legendary magazine *Derrière Le Mirroir* (1946–1982).

Landmark publications were the gothick *Le Corbeau* (1875), Mallarmé's *Un Coup de Dés* (1897), which introduced a spatial framework to poetry, Blaise Cendrars & Sonia Delaunay's pleated *La Prose du Transibérien et la Petite Jehanne de France* (1912), Tristan Tzara & Hans Arp's free-form *Vingt-Cinq Poèmes* (1918), Marcel Duchamp's project notes *La Boîte Verte* (1934), Henri Michaux's *Exorcismes* (1943), André Tal Coat's synaesthetic *Sur Le Pas Du Bouchet* (1959), Samuel Beckett & Jasper John's *Fizzles/Foirades* (1976), and Olivier Debré & Bernard Noël's *Le Livre de L'Oubli* (1985); an extended family of books that graphed the entry into modernity of the sub-genre through the steady demise of the vignette and the notion of illustration as a secondary accompaniment.

French poet Stéphane Mallarmé, 45 years old when he brought out his first de luxe collection, a photolithographic copy of a hand-written manuscript on Japanese vellum, also wrote verse on graph paper. Such innovations would lead to the visual prosody of his last unfinished meta-book *Le Livre*, a seismographic account of his mind, loaded with arcane calculations, a fresh take on the book of nature in which the self-identicality of signs proves an impossible dream, and meaning slips into indeterminacy. *Le Livre* was projected as a kind of literary tomb to bury all the grand idealistic systems of the 19th century, scientific, political, economic and epistemological.[22]

In England, the arts & crafts aesthetic of William Morris's gothic revival Kelmscott Press (attacked by the Italian Futurist Marinetti) can be held responsible for holding back the transformation of the artists' book into a truly modern entity, enshrining a set of design principles in the 1890s (for instance treating wood engraving and letterpress as one synergistic operation) that became decorum for craft-biased artists' book practitioners besotted by the letterpress tendency.

Both Lewis Carroll's *Through the Looking Glass, and What Alice Found There* (1871), and Edwin Abbot's archly entitled *Flatland: A Romance of Many Dimensions* (1884), were phantasmagorias that warped the normal,[23] possessing a topological complexity that looks wildly eccentric when set against the regularising of time necessitated by the spread of the railways, and of course the fully upholstered mid-Victorian novel. They can be read as if analogue 'interfaces' pre-empting the beauty of modern software such as Google Labs Ngrams Viewer, Collex or Devonthink which treat the digital page as a customisable window or stream, allowing you to zoom in, save clippings, underlining or mark ups etc; so re-purposing *tout court*. These enjoyable new forms of reading greatly enlarge Erasmus's notion of textual 'digestibility'.

The fanciful mouse's tail in *Alice in Wonderland* (1865), and new-fangled keyboard *technopeignia* such as secretary Flora F. Stacey's typewriter butterfly,[24] provide evidence of a whimsical, shape-shifting meme, a potential for human 'misuse' embedded in all technology without exception.

3. *Shock Treatment*

Worldbackwards (1912) was the most important publication of The Donkey's Tail collective. Tuned by Velimir Khlebnikov's atavistic polemics to espouse non-Euclidean time and cave painting, it was along with Aleksei Kruchenykh & Olga Rozanova's *Transrational Boog* (1915) an example of a sudden efflorescence of the form between 1910 and 1920. Vasily Komenskii's ferro-concrete poetry in *Tango With Cows* (1914) pointed up a tension between rustic and urban Russia, forces that Kasimir Malevich had instinctively tried to resolve alogistically in his cover artwork for *Threesome* (1913), through the figure of a peasant/robot made of triangles and cones; almost an emblem of the book arts practitioner to come? These diminutive books variously channelled the turbulent energy and aims of Russian Futurism by means of onomatopoeic verse, Cyrillic typography, recycled wallpaper, *Lubki* style woodcut, burlap, carbon copying, hectography, potato or linoleum cuts, fence graffiti and straplines snipped from newspapers, their page sequencing sometimes randomised, so that limited editions were turned into unique runs.

Toned down after the Bolshevik revolution, the look of these crudely fashioned products gradually becomes more austere under the theoretical influence of Soviet Constructivism. Nevertheless during its first period, a tribal cult of 'zaum'[25] prevailed in which rationality was the enemy, Futurism's crude DIY style a contrast to the plush *livres d'artistes* being made at the time in Paris.

Blast (1914–15), was the stridently modern manifesto of Vorticism or the Great English Vortex, a heady brew of Max Stirner's libertarian tract *The Ego and Its Own* (1845), Hermann von Helmholtz's work on fluid mechanics, Henri Bergson's vital élan, and South Sea sensuality, the first multimedia movement in Britain that used abstract art, sculpture and the printed word to systematically attack decaying Edwardian values as exemplified by Roger Fry's Omega workshop in Bloomsbury, ridiculed by leading light Wyndham Lewis.[26]

Blast pulled no punches, a trade union *affiche* that either blasted (e.g. codliver oil, the Post Office, Annie Besant, the Royal Academy) or blessed (e.g. art vandal Frieder Graham, Charlotte Corday, lighthouses, the port of Newcastle). Its idiosyncratic layout featured sans serif block typographic vigour courtesy of the jobbing printers Leveridge & Co., its storm-cone icon and bullet point aggression which critiqued the automobilism of Italian Futurism, and backed women in their fight for universal suffrage, putting forward robust new ideas in sculpture. The hard-edged vertiginous drawings and prints of the Restaurant de la Tour Eiffel crowd, Edward Wadsworth, William Roberts, Jessie Dismorr, Frederick Etchells and Lewis, reveal images threatening to paper surface and surround,[27] the basic urge of most book artists too: antagonism for the limitations of the prim page, the bound codex and thus ancient function of the book as priestly accessory.

Pronounced 'dead' in 1917 by the American poet Ezra Pound, Vorticism has had a key if opaque afterlife as a revolutionary front, influencing such transgressive writers as Kathy Acker, William Burroughs and Stewart Home. But Vorticism's lifespan was cut short by the Great War, indeed two of its members, Henri Gaudier-Brzeska and T. E. Hulme died in combat, the latter blown to pieces by a direct artillery hit. Yet unlike

Cubism, Expressionism, Constructivism and Surrealism that look tired from the standpoint of the 21st century, Vorticism (an ideology that sprang from the Rebel Art Centre) is still fresh and alive in the same way the Big Bang is still happening, although invisible to the naked eye.[28] Together with left-leaning Russian Futurism, it attempted to hijack public taste, generate new vocabularies and tectonically redefine the structure and goal of art, dealing a blow in particular to the idea and practice of genteel illustration.

For all these reasons Vorticism must be cited retrospectively in any account of the artists' book form, which is according to Johanna Drucker an ultra 20th century phenomenon (like oil, information and atonal music), yet one whose paroxysmal phase has now levelled out, normalised even.

4. *Myriad Forms*

Between the end of World War II and the Millennium, the artists' book (despite initially being a form without a proper name), and by implication independent publishing, was an emergent force constructed and deconstructed by a multitude of practitioners, profilers and theorists, integral to the restless agitation of a late anthropocene era that has inexorably seen chic codes enter the mainstream: Situationism, Viennese Aktionism, Auto-Destructive Art, Pop Art, Conceptual Art, Land Art, Mail Art, Systems Theory, Sound Art, Arte Povera, Minimalism, Walking, Dance Performance, Graphic Design, Post-Conceptual Art, Social Art, Food Art, *soi-disant* Art Writing and Post-Internet Art,[29] its key movements that have incrementally contributed to a steady erosion of the specious divide between art and life.

Supercharged significantly during the 1960s and 70s, the artists' book, implicated in language art, moved into alternative space,[30] which saw its insecure status inside the art world slowly dispelled.[31] This self-empowering revolution consisted of several main trends: the vestigial *livre d'artiste* dressed down as typological record, plan chest index or click-shutter photobook, or the concept heavy book as an unfolding locus for radical visiotextual statements,[32] and pulp in the form of self-published, relatively cheap-to-make comics, newspapers or zines. Largely thanks to the influence of Fluxus, Germano Celant and UbuWeb, Sound Art became affiliated. These briefs demonstrated the artists' book as either supplementary to an individual's practice or even a discrete exhibition space, outlier, overflow or site of transaction in itself, focusing unpaid research projects, Fortean dossiers, gonzo texts, drawing-room experiments, hobbyism, crude *barbouillage*, scribble, budget travel diaries, memento mori and blog chatter (types of work often given added value by its privileged individual access); subjective findings translated into delightful, dissenting microcosms, by a designer or impresario able to bypass the hoopla of an exclusive gallery system, and gain a satisfying measure of control over both the distribution and dissemination of their work, even if subject to the noisy demand of public relations. Bringing out an artists' book or multiple has become a smart career move, each one a start-up in itself, a veritable rite of passage.

Take Maurice Lemaitre's Lettrist masterpiece *Roman Hypergraphique* (1950),[33] Andy Warhol's privately printed *A is an alphabet* (1953) with blotted line drawings, Bob Cobbing's pioneering 1950s' experimentation with a Roneo machine and subsequent Punk hollerings, Herman De Vries's *Wit is Overdaad* (1960), Yoko Ono's score-like instruction booklet *Grapefruit: A Book of Instructions and Drawings* (1964), the object heavy 'periodical' *Aspen* (1965–71), a cache of boxed articles, Super-8, and flexidiscs.[34] Take Dennis Oppenheim's board-mounted *Directed Harvest* (1966), Mel Ramsden's art dictionary *Black Book* (1967), Lawrence Weiner's hipsterish art of reader reception theory *Statements* (1968), Nobuyoshi Araki's faintly photocopied *Zerokkusu Shashincho* (1970), Gilbert & George's suave flip-book *Oh, the Grand Old Duke of York* (1972), David Mayor's DIY exhibition in a catalogue *Framed Pieces* (1972), and On Kawara's telegrammatic *I Am Still Alive* (1978). Take Richard Prince's manipulation of mass-market imagery *Tear Sheets* (*c.*1979–1997), Hans-Peter Feldmann's collections of generic photos (e.g. women's knees, snowy mountain tops, footballers etc.) *Bilder* (1968–76), and Christo's mysterious *Wrapped Book* (1978). Take Ernst Caramelle's ultra dry appropriation of newspaper cuttings *Forty Found Fakes* (1979), Frances Butler's confessional *Occult Psychogenic Disturbance* (1980), Henri Chopin's *Typewriter Poems* (1982), and Zero Group member Bernard Aubertin, who equipped flea market books with sulphur matches, fulminate and percussion caps inviting the reader to burn them.[35] Take Les Coleman's *With My Right Hand* (1982) that masquerades as a Silvine exercise book, containing drawings done with his wrong hand, Ernest T's *Cloaca Maxima* (1985–88), an offset litho flyer printed on yellow onion skin paper, Tom Trusky's facsimile *Guest Book* (1992) and Anthony Caro's cardboard pop-up, *Leaf Pool* (1996–2000).

The roll call is virtually endless, the formal diversity mind-boggling, so while it is far too convenient to speak of before and after Celant's

The Book as Artwork 1960–72, the era distinguished by promiscuous signalling and play between disciplines, termed 'intermedia' [36] by Fluxus luminary Dick Higgins in 1966, has explicitly metamorphosed wholesale into one that is now omnipresent, digitally hypermediated and wise to its own gimmicks; meaning the artists' book has blithely surpassed its own definitions en route.

Thus since the term 'artists' book' (allegedly coined by Dianne Perry Vanderlip in 1973[37]), a volcanic eruption has taken place, spreading its plume everywhere, a cloud of formats and multimodal methods (showcased in both the unique artisanal book and limited edition), a longlist including letterpress, pop-up, lasercut, perfect bound, accordion pleat, giclée, risograph, flip, photocopy, stencil, linocut, comb binding, coil binding, monoprint, leporello, Coptic binding, Japanese stitching, silkscreen, CD-ROM, chine collé, rubberstamp, inkjet, serigraph, objet trouvé, Caran d'Ache, pyrography, découpage, clamshell box, secret Belgian binding, telematics, Pompidou binding, transfer print, pin-prick imaging, longstitch, grommets, maps, audio-casette, woodcut, wallet binding, e-scroll, orizome, reliquary, paper carving, acrostics, embroidery, fishbone, folioscope, pochoir, extra-illustration, thermo-chromatic ink, tête-bêche, etching, screw-post binding, erasure and many others.

This seismic shift has seen the emergence of a host of dedicated and exuberant IMPRINTS from Art Metropole and Atlas Press to Book Works, Beau Geste Press and BookRoom, from Café Royal Books, Circle Press and Collective Investigations to Coracle Press, Éditions B42 and Edition Hansjorg Mayer, from The Everyday Press, Fitzcarraldo Editions and Franklin Furnace to Fuel, Granary Books and Heavy Industry Publications, from Iconomoteur, Imschoot Uitgevers and Information as Material to Kaleid Editions, LemonMelon and Monospace Press, from Mörel Books, Occasional Papers and onestar press to Palefroi, Printed Matter and RGAP, from Rollo Press, Sara Ranchouse and Something Else Press to Sternberg Press, Uniformbooks and Valiz, from Very Small Kitchen, Wild Hawthorn Press to Zédélé Éditions.

In their different ways, specialist RETAILERS such as Art Metropole, Boekie Woekie, bookartbookshop, Choisi, Christophe Daviet-Thiery, Claire de Rouen, De Appel, Florence Loewy, Kapsula, Komiyama, PrintRoom, Motto, 6 Decades Books, Trolley Books and X Marks the Bökship have learnt to accommodate a growing consumer appetite for new artists' books and related ephemera, a trend spreading both incrementally and exponentially day in, day out.[38] Often, but not always, shoestring operations, yet commercially astute and with a flair for capturing a niche market, they have considerably broadened the scope and footprint both of individual artists and their outlandish material through in-house commissioning, maintaining a presence at round-the-year trade fairs, running boutique-style galleries or short-lived *galops*, eye-catching web sites and practical hands-on workshops.

Scholarly JOURNALS, MAGAZINES and LEAFLETS concentrating on artists' publications such as *L'Art*, *Book Arts Newsletter*, *The Book on Books on Artists Books*, *Flue*, *J.A.B.*, *Parazine*, *Pages*, *Pop-Up Magazine*, *Print Collector's Newsletter*, *Sans Niveau ni Mètre: Journal du Cabinet du Livre d'Artiste*, *Umbrella*, *Veneer* and *Vivant* plus the online FORUM Artist Books 3.0 have added to the staggering density of this (per)mutable phenomenon, while SITES of excellence, e.g. The Liberated Page Union in Geneva and Centres for Book Arts such as the ones in Minnesota and Saint Yrieix-la-Perche, near Limoges; and the RESEARCH PROGRAMME Les Éditions Incertain Sens, constitute another sign of global popularity.

No survey can be exhaustive, nor would such a listing even be desirable, though many of the publications cited here and way beyond would doubtless have qualified for inclusion in the Vatican's *Index Librorum Prohibitorum*, if it had not been formally closed in 1966 (another victim of the 'permissive' 60s?!).

5. *Whatevernext?*

The parvenu artists' book is part of a substantial ecosystem with a discernible ethnographic affinity to and family resemblance with board games, automata, music boxes and Pelham Puppets, the art of tying knots, knitting, Tunbridge Wells marquetry and cabinet making, tramp art, *le style trash*, origami and Vaudeville paper tearing, chits, dingbats, microscopic writing and cryptography, the Marseilles tarot, indecipherable weather diaries, Xerox machines, commonplace cut & paste[39] and furniture bodging, hand-held home video, Post-Its, death masks, Nang Yai and silhouette portaiture, entomology, palmistry, sand sculpture, twisters, the cycles of the moon and early-modern rogue pamphlets, rebus, Albrecht Dürer's *Melencholia I*, 1514, the Fugger newsletter, non-conformist tracts and broadsides, 419 Letters, analogue card indexes and Victorian plantsman's catalogues, wrongteous quack remedies, psychogeography, Zeppelins and cadastral rolls, runic divination, paper money, Mexican chocolate skulls and speaking in

Enochian tongues, Dada, Bluetooth, Pooh sticks, crop circles, boarding-house black magic and planchettes, bottle dumps, yard sales, Congolese nail fetishes, pelmanism, foraging and cooking wild food, Jackass type practical jokes, futiques, snow globes, shanty house construction and Sugru©, PNG kula, malanggan, gulag tattooing, bakelite, nursery rhymes, deaf signing, flash fiction and Romany caravans, flarf, follies, Esperanto, nautical charts, silk POW maps and out-of-date travel brochures, faxes, PechaKucha 20x20, Poincaré time, mis-pselt street signage and architectural schematics,[40] superstrings, LEGO©, operating instructions of all kinds, Poundland, Edward Lear's nonsense ditties, Tauchnitz Editions, cloudscapes and free newspapers, shopping lists, trance states, yellow literature, trench art and jest books, nursery rhymes, *Old Moore's Almanac*, consumer surveys, questionnaires, junk mail, lost cat notices, *faits divers*, semaphore and QR codes, hopscotch, the Cottingley fairy hoax, Braille dot matrix, tachygraphy, *papillotes*, and sewing bees, hopscotch, football fanzines, rubbish of every kind, dirt, dust, soot and ink blots, in short a plethora of impure, elastic forms and oft disregarded vernacular formats, rhopographic yet profound too.

Charged with data management tasks & duties, the smart phone and personal computer have taken a load off the conventional book, simultaneously enabling the artists' book to become an off-road stealth vehicle roving interdisciplinary space, a new branch of sculpture (see Appendix I) as much as literary text, its fabrication taking place in a constant whirl of materials, means, and applications. Furthermore, a largely DIY driven ethos was intensified and accelerated by the advent of the world wide web in 1993, which duly triggered an identity crisis in mainstream publishing, and coincided with a new era of virile self-publishing, making the genre-fuzzy, contemporary artists' book an objective site of empowerment, re-skilling and hybridity.

Another contemporary trend is decentralised design and publishing. Collate, a project set up by James Cuddy and Roma Levin, installed touch-screens at the V&A,[41] allowing visitors to tag Instagram images and layout spreads. These were then voted on by users and a finished book printed, one snapshot of an upending of the traditional linear model of publishing; authorship replaced by algorithm. Collective Dissent, a group project by year 2 BA Fine Art students at Central Saint Martins, London, investigated collaborative practice, pooling solo work to build and extract brand new compilations. Any pages printed off could then be fed back into a printer by onlookers, blurry palimpsests of the entire event.[42]

The IMP BrainCandy that encourages its users or 'artisans' to generate content in a communal online space made its network debut with *The Runes of Gallidon: Discover a World, Forge its Future* (2009)[43] featuring podcasts, flash games etc.

In the wake of R. B. Kitaj's screenprint series of worn book jackets *In Our Time: Covers for a Small Library After the Life for Most Part*, 1969, superbly remade by Goshka Macuga as *After In Our Time*, 2011, such cover art has become a part of book arts. Other adepts are Jamie Shovlin, who in *Fontana Modern Masters*, 2005, a homage to the stylish 1970s paperbacks, completed the series by inventing geometric watercolour covers for its ten lost books, Harland Miller whose loft-friendly treatments of Penguin jackets are in great demand, Martin McGinn who pre-vandalises pages from art history books before painting them in oil as scrunched up Dutch *Vanitas*, Mark Fraser-Betts' delicate retropulp, and John Hilliard's *Cover Stories* consisting of photographic enlargements of monochrome areas on jackets recomposed into blocks of colour and overlaid on images of books.

Thanks variously to the fully searchable digitised databases generated by Google Books,[44] Project Gutenberg, Million Book Project, and the Open Content Alliance, many tatty secondhand volumes have come to be seen as disposable, late books so to speak, begging to be modified.[45] Paradoxically the history of the book with a stress on its materiality has emerged as a bone fide academic discipline with important centres at Princeton, Edinburgh, Toronto, London and Hong Kong, flagging up book studies as far more than a voguish reflex to technological change.[46]

6. *Broken Rules & Parameters*

John Latham's notorious interventions abusing the book as material object rather than text, and their terminus in his burning 'skoob' towers, paved the way psychologically for many practitioners of today. Latham's overpainted book reliefs, such as *Burial of Count Orgaz*, 1958, emit a strong sense of disturbance as if an electrically charged nerve had been cut out and laid bare on a table. The term is apt, since many of these unpretty pieces are table-like, altars hefted up onto the wall plane; microlibraries rather than individual books. The key issue addressed and tackled by Latham, though, was sacrilege and thus the subject's troubled relationship to discourses of morality and power, and how these are grammatically inscribed, and policed from within, a thematic which has turned into a focus of the artists' book in general.

Unhampered by censorship or authoritarian discourse, a desire for the sublime paradoxically arrived at through the abject has meant a whole new generation of extreme book art practitioners such as Cara Barer (immersion), David Blackmore (fluorescent highlighting), Jonathan Callan (relief carving), Egidija Ciricaite (pseudo-bookbinding), Nicola Dale (knowledge reformatting), Emanuel Dundic (perforation), Michael Hampton (morphing) Nicci Haynes (shredding), Samantha Huang (découpage), Sarah Jacobs (extraordinary rendition), Naomi Kashiwagi (gramaphonics), Jacqueline Rush Lee (petrification), Christina Mitrentese (target practice), Kristen Mueller (textual removal), the Rimbaudian seekers of lice (minor poetry),[47] Finlay Taylor (entomobooks) and Elisabeth Tonnard (invisibility), are neither bothered any more by ancient taboos about damaging books (or shellac discs), nor speeding up their end as intact objects, the call to 'stress test to destruction' often a *sine qua non*. What would once have been seen as banned activity not only implies a challenge to the 'No Pens Policy' of COPAC research libraries, but causes a creative ripple and indispensable rethink in the aesthetic field of connoisseurship too.

Quirky publications such as Karin Ruggaber's *Villas* (2010), a photobook of new Roma houses, Urs Odermatt's *Karambolage* (2003), a collection of Swiss car crash stills and High Chair Editions' *Trampolines and Bouncy Castles* (2013), keep the non-pedagogic, taxonomic album tradition of the Bechers alive and well. Paul Buck's *A Public Intimacy (a life through scrapbooks)* (2011) adopts a related, obliquely autobiographical idiom that preserves the past through facsimiles of grainy Fleet Street cuttings and lists of book/film reviews and celebrity obits. Appropriation, a controversial topic deserving a book all to itself, is marvellously represented by Swedish artist Carl Johan De Geer via a series of classic crime novel tweaks, such as his treatment of Peter Cheyney's *I'll Say She Does* (1945), *Det Brann Inte Alls* (2010). Fiona Banner's indian ink wall text *Black Hawk Down*, 2010, her *récit* of Ridley Scott's eponymous war flick, draws on the osmosis between big screen cinema and its consumption, a scrawled tale of the remix era that sidesteps copyright issues with bravado. Dimitri Prigov and Mikhail Pogaresky have renewed the Russian Futurist season ticket too.

A conceptual lineage is served by Colin Sackett's commandeerings, Art & Language's paperchains *Portraits of a Dream* (2009), Simon Lewty's fake chancery manuscripts and Inga Kerber's *Catalogue Raisonné (Clichés)* (2014). Another strain of neo-conceptualism rests with Claire Fontaine, who takes her name from a brand of French notebooks, and Sarah

Mackillop who produces stationery based work such as *50 Envelope Windows* (2008), and found textual reprints. Her *Modern Art in Everyday Life* (2011) documents a trail of zoomorphic doodles left behind by an unimpressed reader on top of the original booklet, whilst Peter Piller's *Zeitung* (2007), an archive of crap images from ATMs and CCTV, pastiches Aby Warburg's legendary *Bilderatlas*! The collaborative doing and undoing of Marjorie Welish & James Siena finds its lyrical apotheosis in *Oaths? Questions?* (2009). Viennese-based Anatol Knopek's huge online archive *Visual-Poetry* ably documents the dynamic, ever-changing world of VisPo, such as Philip Adrian's four volume data realisation >>*#oneSecond 09.11.12 14:47:36 GMT* (2013), recording over 5,000 simultaneous tweets worldwide. Spineless Classics publishes the entire text of novels such as *Wuthering Heights* or *1984* on A0 posters.

7. *Other Resources*

In the case of children's literature, pastimes and games, there is a noticeable tension between *dulcis et utile* or pleasure and instruction. This meant that as the child slowly emerged as an independent consumer, a process hand-in-hand with the boom in print culture of the late 18th century onwards, their reading matter—'penny plain and tuppence coloured'—was characterised by an underlying dialectic shaping both form and content; one geared towards the agendas of personal improvement and entry into polite society.

The chapbook, or miniature collection of verses with 'cuts', i.e. block printed or copper-plate illustrations, was a vehicle both of fun as well as cautionary fable, its vocabulary of doggerel, quips, trifles, hints, prattle, ballads, valentines, and jingles mobilised to teach healthy pursuits and sports such as skating, cricket, peg-top, leapfrog, hoop-bowling, dressing dolls and marbles as well as correct manners and deportment, for the discrete realm of children's literature is a fluid and complex one that absorbs, appropriates and assimilates whatever it fancies.

From his shop at 65 St Paul's Churchyard, the quack doctor John Newbery[48] published landmark titles such as *A Little Pretty Pocket Book etc* (1744), with its courtesy pincushion and ball, and *The History of Little Goody Two-Shoes* (1769), which despite its sententious messages about virtue and vice remained a firm favourite in the nursery for the next hundred and fifty years.[49] This nascent market was given greater definition by *The Juvenile Magazine* (1788), and Sunday School m'am

Mrs Trimmer's review *The Guardian of Education* (1802–1806), while Ann Taylor—one of a pair of influential and pious sisters from Ongar in Essex—authored *Signor Topsy-Turvy's Wonderful Magic Lantern: or, The World Turned Upside Down* (1810) with its hint of fantastic scenarios to come in the world of KinderLit; Elizabeth Turner's cloying verses in *The Cowslip* (1811) charmed even as they moralised.

Then there were didactic primers such as *Punctuation Personified: or Pointing Made Easy, by Mr Stops* (1824), with its hilarious figures formed from circumflexes, brackets and exclamation marks etc, D. Carvalho's *The Life and Death of an Apple Pie* (*c*.1830), and *Traditional Nursery Songs of England* (1843), compiled by Henry Cole—the inventor of the Christmas card. The late Victorian epoch was dominated by publishing firms such as Thomas Nelson & Sons, whose *Clever Cats* (1881) still delights today when pet cats can be internet stars, Raphael Tuck & Sons, with its trade catalogue of postcards, puzzles, and pull-the-tab movable books, but above all Frederick Warne & Co., who promoted illustrators such as Randolph Caldecott and Kate Greenaway, although it was Beatrix Potter's unmistakable books beginning with *The Tale of Peter Rabbit* (1902) that made the company synonymous with fine art literature for children.[50]

The Great War interrupted the flow of novelties from Germany aimed at young readers, e.g. Ernest Nister's panoramas and Lothar Meggendorfer's trick books and peep shows, so it wasn't till the 1930s that the pop-up book (a term coined by Harold Lentz) would have its heyday, particularly in the Bookano series, although paper cutting and scenography[51] has been reborn in the 21st century graphic design studio, facilitated by laser technology.

So the tropes of childrens' literature have fed the unconscious of the contemporary artists' book, as did the allegorical comic which despite being hampered by its non-fine art lineage, and therefore labelled taxonomically "awkward" by Clive Phillpot,[52] with its content of cellular speech bubbles, fast paced lurid action, generic pre-requisite of suspended disbelief in fanatical readers, and *dramatis personae* of morally simplified characters or superheroes, deserves to be reconsidered even if only at the edge of the pantheon.

Ranging from the so-called penny dreadfuls[53] with their 'fierce' cover images, to the *Illustrated London News* (1842–2013), *The Magnet* (1908–1940), (particularly its 'red phase', 1908–15) the indestructible *Beano* (1938–), *Weird Tales* (1923–54/1988–2013), the moral panic inducing *Tales from the Crypt* (1954), *Giles* (1946), Frank Hampson's superb illustrations adorning the rotogravure printed *Eagle* (1950–1969/1982–1994), and Robert Crumb's edgy *Fritz the Cat* (1959–1972). From Chicago caretaker and reclusive weather man Henry Darger's *The Story of the Vivian Girls, in What is Known as the Realms of the Unreal, of the Glandeco-Angelinian War Storm, Caused by the Child Slave Rebellion* (n.d.), to the photo-strips of the hugely successful *Viz* (1979), Alan Moore & Eddie Campbell's occult influenced chiller *From Hell* (1989–1996), Hergé's *The Adventures of Tintin* (1929), Raymond Pettibon's dystopic west coast imagery, and the re-purposing of The Numbskulls in Steven Warwick's *Interiors* (2013). From French freak scene publishing house Le Dernier Cri, with its sassy boast of "grafic infection since 1993"[54], Seth Grahame-Smith's schlock mash-up *Pride and Prejudice and Zombies* (2009), Japanese Manga, Anime, Super Deformed and ergotic Souzou scrapbooks, and a veritable slew of desk top published zines and cheap Xeroxed underground bulletins to the Neoists of the '80s and '90s, to OuBaPo member Etienne Lécroart's *Bande Dessinée de Möbius* (2008). From the American libertarian wing represented by Mike Gunderloy's[55] spirit duplicated *Factsheet Five* (1982–1991), the subversive ideas of Messrs Bob Black and Hakim Bey, *Punk*, Christian Greer's *Journal for the Study of Horseplay, Hijinx, And Tomfoolery* (2012), and Jay Potts smoking webcomic *World of Hurt: The Thrill Seekers* (2011) to Turkish *Apricot City A4* (2010) that took its title from a mobile photocopier/PVC lamination cart, the London-based post-colonial arty biannual *Schizm* (2010), the Hubert Kretschmer Archive of zines, Museo Universitario del Chopo's Fanzinoteca archive, and Marvel's *Young Avengers* (2013), to Peter Rapp's grotesque Peakean chavbooks.

The comic book business is irrepressible, and has been given critical kudos by the British Library's major retrospective exhibition 'Comics Unmasked: Art & Anarchy in the UK'.[56] Without evangelising, this demonstrated how only critical snobbism has caused them to be consistently denigrated by brickbats such as low brow, seditious, popular and disposable. Yet even in their mass-produced form, an editorial commitment to quality draughtsmanship, and a discernible if sometimes dark and gruesome poesis means that the American funny, the comic strip, aka Franco-Belgian *bande dessinée*, the comic book, *fumetto*, latterday graphic novel and web-comic constitute a notable part of the territory designated 'pulp modernism' by David M. Earle, the comic format's fluid imbrication of visual and verbal tropes *qua* audience favourites, making it worthy of serious consideration under the liberal yet contested rubric of the opuscular artists' book, rather than merely trash literature from the wrong side of the tracks.

The English proto-ecologist Gilbert White's initial diary *Garden Kalendar* (1751–1768) was a book of cheap hand-stitched quarto letter paper, while its sequel *The Natural History and Antiquities of Selborne, in the County of Southampton* (1789) detailed a secure vision of natural life's pattern in which *Homo sapiens* was confidently perched on top of the evolutionary ladder, a viewpoint vulnerable to the cognitive hammerblows dealt by Charles Lyell's *Principles of Geology* (1830), Charles Darwin's *On the Origin of Species by Means of Natural Selection* (1859), and Alexander von Humboldt's überbuch *Kosmos* (1845–1862). Today *The Whole Earth Catalogue* (1968–72), Mark Dion's indexical bier *Scala Naturae* (1994), Helen Douglas's moody photo book *Wild Wood*[57] (1999), Sarah Bodman's *G.M. Future* (1999), a faux-corporate report about plant manipulation and Jason Clark's grungy drawings of vehicles slowly being subsumed by rampant vegetation *Driven-Out, Ditched & Deserted* (2008),[58] continue the eco-idiom. Katie Paterson's black map of nearly 27,000 dead stars *All the Dead Stars* (2009), Benedict Drew's duffer's chemistry experiment with air, carbon, calcium and water *How I Failed to Make Man* (2011), *Doggerland* (2012) the first part of the Submerged Territories series, Pauline Lamont-Fisher's leporello book *Aconbury Walk* (2013), Sarah Jacobs' self-published[59] *After Nature: Highlights* (2014), a decomposed article from *Nature* journal and the Strange Attractor book/CD *Animal Music* (2015) which reveals an exotic soundworld, and Ryoji Ikeda's *Datamatics* (2006), an immersive audiovisual extravaganza based on binary codes, all go to show the indisputable presence of a cosmological thematic refracted through an ineffable *terroir*—the final Kaprowesque collapse of the categories 'art' and 'nature'[60] exposed as unstable and subject to Marx's 'metabolic rift'.

Be it collections of pressed flowers and ferns, the classic pocket field guide format, more-conversational pond notes and hedgerow queries or *aurora borealis* holiday snaps, as the scientific probing of cosmic nature has grown more vertiginous and bewildering, the innate flexibility of the artists' book particularly since the digital turn allows its technicians either to hearken back to these publishing stalwarts or adopt and redo them with a modern twist, insinuating their category-busting products amongst an avalanche of koolkunst coffee table ISBNs.

This *excursus* demonstrates how a grammatically unruly species is no freak mutation.

'Conclusion'

Contemporary production processes and methodology tap into the rich mix of all the potentialities trapped in Ice Age artefacts, scrolls, the antique codex[61] and post 1440 Gutenberg printed tome, so long responsible for preserving orthodox[62] religious belief or Enlightenment scientific knowledge. A growing bio-diversity of opuscular objects in an increasingly post-scriptural age has many that do not resemble books any more, their digital text- and image-content on a par; altermodern, low-church kits or ergodic reading experiences offering 'très riches heures' to readers/users; not a protected species, an artisan item only available at book fairs.

For reports of the book's demise have proved untrue, as *The Book is Alive!* (2013) asserts. This important conference[63] round-up addressed the impact of digital technologies on the interdisciplinary book, or the re-invention of the artists' book in an age of enhanced e-reading,[64] the death of the editor, DRM and POD.[65] Fortunately the prognosis looks good, since the pathway from book as site to book as website is two-way, and interactive 'page turning' a cinch without actual pages when conducted on an infinite screen plane. Now fun-with-words videos on YouTube signal the possibility for a boundless textuality Stéphane Mallarmé could not have dreamt of.

The digestible artists' book (i.e. liable to dog-earing, nicks, even the occasional hand-written marginal annotation), since no longer circumscribed by art world protocols[66] is fast becoming steganographically indistinguishable from the age-old diptychal book itself, which has also been forced to give ground and undergo the adaptation of its content in order to tap into new audiences and make the most of backlit, handheld reading technologies; so much so that it in future it will not be so easy to tell the difference between an artists' book and a flexibound or stitched casebound book since the wall between them has been irrevocably broken down creating a mixed super category, the artists' book revealed to have been the estimable VECTOR[67] of a far grander human project: nothing less than the full flowering and apotheosis of the book itself, or in Timothy Morton's language an unsurpassable "hyperobject",[68/69] an integrated bulk bibliographic carrier of unknowable,[70] speculative and known knowledge, an überarchive, open unshelfmarked library and plastic reflection of our own neurological 're-wiring' as internet users, citizens of the worldwide albeit panoptic web,[71] living with the hypothetical and scary possibility of one networked global consciousness.[72]

Yet as this spatio-temporal vector slowly decomposes and loses identity, track marks of its diversifying effect remain behind, making its complex story mappable.[73] The still active archival traces of its epigenetic role (species revenge upon genus!) in an ongoing human drama are tougher to evaluate though, as both the material (handy) and virtual (roamable) democratised object change.[74] Nevertheless the morphic resonance of the embalmable entity 'artists' book' continues to subtly vibrate across the transdisciplinary mediascape of learning, cutting-edge thought, news and entertainment, no longer elitist or confined to any particular *habitus*.

Unshelfmarked celebrates this highly dynamic, disruptive state of affairs.[75]

Notes

1 He has been criticised by Mœglin-Delcroix for "...a narrowly conceptual interpretation of the artist's book", Anne Mœglin-Delcroix et al, *Looking Telling, Thinking, Collecting: Four Directions of the Artist's Book from the Sixties to the Present* (Mantua: Edizioni Corraini, 2006), p.37. From the outset Celant was more interested in their unlimited potential as communication tools rather than fetishises.

2 Nigel Greenwood Inc. Ltd, London SW1, 25 November–21 December 1972.

3 Retrospectively Mœglin-Delcroix made 1962 her annus mirabilis for the still unbaptised form.

4 Phillpot's diagram made for *Artforum*, vol.20, no.9, May 1972, p.77, that attempted to shed light on the meaning of various terms used to define the artists' book, a venture refined in notes to *Outside of a Dog: Paperbacks and Other Books by Artists*, Baltic, Gateshead, 27 September–30 May 2003/4, only certified the old adage *obscurius per obscurem*.

5 Carrión's definition: "...books in which the book form, a coherent sequence of pages, determines conditions of reading that are intrinsic to the work", in 'Bookworks Revisited', *The Print Collector's Newsletter*, vol.2, no.1, March–April 1980, p.8, remains the most useful and nuanced.

6 To be fair, Perée sees in the artists' book "...a delightful contrariness", 'Introduction: Old Loves and New Insights', *Cover to Cover: The Artist's Book in Perspective* (Rotterdam/Breda: NAi and De Beyerd, 2002), p.11.

7 Wikipedia tentatively cites the *Book of Kells* (*c*.800 AD) and *Les Très Riches Heures du Duc de Berry* (1412–16) as "precursors" of the artists' book. http://en.wikipedia.org/wiki/Artist_book

8 Blake was mocked by Wyndham Lewis as "...our arch-Policeman", *Blast* (1914), p.137.

9 "Books are objects that conjoin openness and closure together, like the hands to which they belong", Andrew Piper, *Book Was There* (2012), p.4.

10 Marcus Walsh, "Books are crafted objects, embodying critical intelligence, made by the normally irreversible decisions of their authors, printers and publishers", 'Theories of Text, Editorial Theory, and Textual Criticism', *The Oxford Companion to the Book*, vol.1 (Oxford: Oxford University Press, 2010), p.163.

11 *Private Eye*, no.1355, 13–20 December 2013, p.18.

12 Will our own razor thin Wi-Fi tablets one day be left abandoned, flat-batteried epitaphs for archaeologists of the future to puzzle over?

13 I am indebted to Craig Dworkin for this signifier.

14 "En une rêverie de solitude qui accroît la solitude du rêveur, deux profondeurs se conjuguent, se répercutent en échos qui vont de la profondeur de l'être du monde à une profondeur d'être du rêveur. Le temps est suspendu. Le temps n'a plus d'hier et n'a plus de demain. Le temps est englouti dans la double profondeur du rêveur du monde." Gaston Bachelard, *La Poétique de la Rêverie* (Paris: Presses Universitaires de France, 1974), p.148.

15 Dr John Dee's scryer, Edward Kelley may have fabricated the manuscript to swindle Rudolf II.

16 Started in 2003, the Cambridge Illuminations Research Project is cataloguing some 4000 illuminated western manuscripts and incunabula at the Fitzwilliam Museum and the Cambridge Colleges.

17 "His radical revision of Romantic landscape—the solitary wanderer confronting the unpeopled view—consists of an even more extreme version of its traditional exclusions", Tom Lubbock, 'Richard Long: Walks on the Wild Side', *The Independent*, 2 June 2009.

18 Respectively the starting points for contemporary exhibitions devised by the Laurence Sterne Trust.

19 In an interview Anna Gerber and Britt Iverson, aka 'Visual Editions' regret the way "...the book has come out in so many different editions since it was first published, that it's completely lost its magic and playfulness along the way. So what we wanted to do was to dust it down from its shoddy Dover classics and make the book relevant and contemporary again". www.itsnicethat.com/articles/3100-visual-editions

20 "The overturning of this paradigm" is described by Clive Phillpot in 'Strong Shadow, Much Light', exhibition notes to Arnaud Desjardin's, 'Comma 38', Bloomberg Space, London EC2, 14 July–18 September 2011. However, *livres d'artistes* (not unlike Books of Hours) need to be viewed as a highly articulate evolutionary phase, and not used as a left-winger's Aunt Sally.

21 "Drawing plus writing is a whole new *way* of thinking. It is where we become categorically different", Piper, *op. cit.*, p.78.

22 Mallarmé's notes first appeared in a music journal dedicated to serialism, *Die Reihe*, no.6, 1960, where several leading American artists came across them.

23 Hermann von Helmholtz had shown in the 1850s and 60s that Euclidean axioms were only partially true.

24 *Pitman's Phonetic Journal*, 15 October 1898.

25 Literally the moment just before dawn, or pre-rational consciousness.

26 A "...curtain and pincushion factory in Fitzroy Square", *Blast: War Number* (London: John Lane, 1915), p.41.

27 This vertigo was experienced first-hand by Wyndham Lewis: "I seized Hulme by the throat; but he transfixed me upon the railings of Soho Square. I never see the summer house in its centre without remembering how I saw it upside down." *Blasting and Bombardiering* (London: John Calder, 1982), p.36.

28 See Ami Clarke's review of 'The Vorticists: Manifesto for a Modern World', Tate Britain, London SW1, 14 June–4 September 2011. www.a-n.co.uk/interface/reviews/single/1800877

29 Basically as Jörg Heiser has commented "...any kind of chic that promises an aura of subversion". www.frieze.com/issue/article/industrial_relations

30 Whilst acknowledging this broadening out and infiltration by the artists' book, a sceptical Les Coleman bemoaned "...the institutionalised setting up of specialist courses for their study, creating a vogue, rather like public art, for practice rather than serving any purpose". www.bookarts.uwe.ac.uk/coleman.htm

31 No longer "...a side-line of the principal activities of painters... or sculptors" as in Clive Phillpot's memorable phrase, 'Recent Art and the Book Form', *Artist's Books: From the Traditional to the Avant-Garde* (New Brunswick, NJ: Rutgers University, 1982), p.2.

32 Against "...a backdrop of social unrest and street politics", Sam Demircan, 'Clive Phillpot: Booktrek', *Art Monthly*, no.377, June 2014.

33 Unfairly described by Joanna Drucker as "...completely unintelligible", *The Century of Artists' Books* (New York: Granary, 1995), p.230.

34 In her editorial for *Aspen*, no.1, Phyllis Johnson stressed how "...a bit of rock, wildflower seeds, tea samples, an opera libretti [sic], old newspapers, jigsaw puzzles" would have been perfectly acceptable contents too.

35 See my 'Strike a Light: The Incendiary Practice of Bernard Aubertin, Né 1934'. www.slashseconds.co.uk/michael-hampton/13/64/146/submission/strike-a-light/

36 http://www.artpool.hu/Fluxus/Higgins/intermedia2.html

37 See Foreword to the exhibition catalogue for the Vanderlip organised 'Artists Books', Moore College of Art, Philadelphia, 23 March–30 April 1973.

38 Offprint London, a book fair held in the Turbine Hall, Tate Modern, London, 22–25 May 2015, showcased the rude health of contemporary publishing.

39 See Stephen Johnson's Hearst New Media lecture, 2010 'The Glass Box and the Commonplace Book'. www.stevenberlinjohnson.com/2010/04/the-glass-box-and-the-commonplace-book.html

40 www.nycsubway.org

41 The London Design Festival, 14–22 September 2013. www.vimeo.com/94662099

42 Banner Repeater, London E5, 27 May 2014.

43 www.runesofgallidon.com

44 Thanks to superfast turnover using infra red cameras and OCR technology, Google Books passed 30 million scanned and digitised books in 2013.

45 'Perversions of Paper' was a workshop and symposium organised by the Material Texts Network at Birkbeck College, London WC1, in the summer of 2014. www.perversionsofpaper.com

46 According to Gill Partington "...this separation of writing and paper has not ushered in the End of the Book, as once predicted. In the age of its supposed technological obsolescence, the book has become something rich and strange, emerging in all its papery singularity". www.lrb.co.uk/blog/2014/05/06/gill-partington/the-invisible-book

47 "...a bid to eschew resolution and the want to be major, influential, great, serious, monumental, superior", press release to 'Encyclops' at news of the world, London SE8, 29 November–15 December 2013.

48 "He published books which were immediately attractive to children: in a small format, with illustrations, and bound in brightly-coloured flowered paper." www.bl.uk/reshelp/findhelpsubject/literature/chillit/childhist/childhistorical.html

49 Jane Austen left a battered miniature copy at her death, bound with gilt and flowered Dutch boards.

50 'Nursery Classics: Frederick Warne Fine Art Picture Books', NAL, V&A, 3 February–11 May 2015.

51 Andreas Johansson keeps the handmade pop-up tradition alive in his free zone landscapes such as *From Where the Sun Now Stands* (2011), a species of 'microbibliotecture'.

52 'Books by Artists and Books as Art' in *Booktrek: Selected Essays on Artists' Books* (Zurich/Dijon: JRP Ringier and Les Presses du Reél, 2013), p.201.

53 Their mass production and circulation was dramatically enlarged by the invention of the paper-making machine and rotary steam printing press.

54 www.derniercrinews.blogspot.co.uk

55 "His 'Factsheet Five' Collection of over 10,000 zines and mail art is now held at the New York State Library in Albany, New York, where it occupies 300 cubic feet ($8.5m^3$)". www.en.wikipedia.org/wiki/Mike_Gunderloy

56 2 May–19 August 2014.

57 http://www.artistsbooksonline.org/works/wiwo/imageindex/1.1.1.0.xml

58 "The cars, abandoned along old logging roads, ditched down ravines, driven in up to their wheel-wells in sand-pits, burned and bullet ridden, and left to disintegrate and then integrate into nature." Jason Clark, *Driven-Out, Ditched & Deserted* (Clonmel: Coracle, 2008).

59 Thankfully the stigma that was once attached to vanity or self-publishing has now largely evaporated.

60 Jenny Uglow goes so far as to pedantically claim "The natural world itself is, it seems an artists' book", reviewing *Of Green Leaf, Bird and Flower: Artists' Books and the Natural World* in *The British Art Journal*, vol.XV, no.1, (2014).

61 The Coptic book perhaps most closely resembles our modern version.

62 Apart perhaps from Buckminster Fuller's room size *Tetra Scroll* (1975–77), the artists' book has steered clear of the gigantism which afflicts much so called 'post-medium' art.

63 BOOKLIVE! International Symposium, London South Bank University, London SE1, 8–9 June, 2012.

64 Typically "…sound tracks, pop-up windows, and moving images", Piper, *op. cit.*, p.46.

65 In Emmanuelle Waeckerlé's telling phrase, an "…interplay between pixel and page", 'A Few Introductory Thoughts', *The Book is Alive!* (Sheffield: RGAP, 2013), p.7.

66 It is quite likely a perceived lack of art historical baggage, i.e. male ontology, that has made book arts in the widest sense of the term, so attractive to female practitioners.

67 This usage carries several connotations, including that of a quantity with magnitude and force, an organism, such as a pollinator, and an agent, for example plasma carrying exogenous genes designed to alter a genome.

68 That is "…entities of such vast temporal and spatial dimensions that they defeat traditional ideas about what a thing is in the first place". www.upress.umn.edu/book-division/books/hyperobjects

69 Tauba Auerbach's *[2, 3]* (2011), six die-cut sculptures in a slipcase takes the artists' book to a new level, especially in terms of paper engineering.

70 In Renaissance cartography, uncharted areas were annotated with the Latin tag *hic sunt dracones*.

71 Where being a user leaves us open to the scrutiny of those who administer each level of service provision.

72 According to Raymond Kurzweil "The Singularity" will take place in 2045.

68 See Radoslaw Nowakowski's ABTREE diagram. www.bookarts.uwe.ac.uk/projects/canon.html

73 Cham's *Democritisation de l'art*, a cartoon squib of Courbet's famous painting *The Stonebreakers*, 1849, depicts two quarrymen in preposterous, oversized clogs. *L'illustration*, 21 July 1855.

74 "Permanence? Stability! I can't believe it's gone", Ford Madox Hueffer, 'The Saddest Story', *Blast* (1914), p.88.

Literaturwurst

Dieter Roth, 1961
—newspaper, spices

To single out one representative piece of work from the extraordinarily diverse, multi-faceted oeuvre of Dieter Roth is in itself child's play, yet also a kind of violation of the vast, uncontrollable moving mass of this man who had the calm yet intense demeanour of a pork butcher. Linocut, woodcut, etching, copperplate engraving, aquatint, offset litho, screenprint, rubber-stamps, overpainted postcards, monotype letterpress, puzzles, unique and multiple artists' books, concrete poetry, diaries, hoarder's ring-binders, table ruins, food sculpture, and video[1] were some of the media that he chose to investigate, his *nachlass* not unlike the solidified volcanic magma of Roth's adopted home Iceland. Other activities included setting up the business Hotelkunst AG to promote his wares, and an early type of 'art on demand'; while he pursued significant collaborations with Richard Hamilton, Stefan Wewerka and Arnulf Rainer among others.

Born in Hanover in 1930 of Swiss German parents, he was fostered to a family of hoteliers in Zurich in 1943, and yet that early geographical connection with Kurt Schwitters and the site of the original Merzbau appears to have been a subliminal influence throughout Roth's life, and it makes rudimentary sense to classify his output as neo-Merz, possessing that very strong Schwitters-like sense of art as something made in and of the household, exploiting quotidian or reject materials:

> "…the uglier it is the better".[2]

Roth became renowned for his highly unorthodox sculptural deployment of foodstuffs, particularly sausage, bread, cheese, cocoa powder, cinnamon and sugar, such inherently unstable materials being the source of many subsequent curatorial headaches, while raising tough questions about the shelflife of art objects, and subverting notions of the immortal statement by means of the explicit unmanageable whiff of rot and decay.[3]

Literaturwurst itself belongs to this cadre of unspeakable gastroart, the first in a notorious series begun in 1961 that would culminate in 1974 with a slaughterhouse installation Frankfurtering the complete works of Hegel. Roth's salami sausages would be stuffed with real gelatine, lard, garlic and spices as well as ground up printed matter, which ranged from the *Daily Mirror* to *Quick*, *Bunte*, *Der Spiegel*, and *Stern*.

Bon appetit.

---

1 Notably *Solo Scenes*, 1998, "...a different videotaped slice of Roth's daily activity in his studios in Iceland, Basel and Hamburg, on different days during the last year of his life when he was overcoming alcoholism and heart disease and knew that his time was limited". David Briers, 'Dieter Roth 'Diaries'', *Art Monthly*, no.359, September 2012.

2 Motto from *Flat Waste*, *c*.1975.

3 Letter from the author to the editor, *Tate Research Papers* 8, Autumn 2007: Replication. "The paradox of seeing a Roth in a museum is certainly a significant aspect of its reception, and clearly the artist was savvy to the problematic his output would bring to museums, as it challenges their fundamental mindset and reason for being by its sheer processuality. So, museums and private collectors are faced with a tricky choice between fetishising objects till they literally stink the place out... or realising that the asymptotic line from their creator has actually reached an end, and that there is most definitely a point at which entropic intervention turns them into sad piles of waste. Now that is a tough call to make, a critical aesthetic judgement, but a radical call that might be made somewhat easier by the following three factors:
i. An acknowledgement that the performative lifetime of the work is over, and that the buyer has 'had their money's worth'.
ii. That sufficient high-quality photographic documentation, or archival blueprints etc. exist, in case there is a demand to re-make the 'original'.
iii. That destruction opens up museal space for new cultural statements/artefacts."

Living For Less

Linda Toigo, 2012
—modified book

The raw material for Linda Toigo's *Living For Less* is as matter of fact as it gets. Confronted by hundreds of brand new Spring/Summer 2012 Argos catalogues piled up on wooden pallets in store, she has simply purloined one for her own ends; a shopper with a hidden agenda.

The appropriation lacks controversy, but this is not the issue, as equipped with non-sterile surgical blades, bone folder, cutting mat and a great deal of patience Toigo's underhand strategy is pre-conceived: a highly calculated alteration of both physical integrity and illustrative logic contained in a shopper's 'bible', one that neutralises the catalogue's almost ritualistic function as a themed list of product serial numbers, hardware which with a completed order form and cash or credit card can be made to materialise at a collection point, as if the thaumaturgy of a handbook venerated by a bewitched High Street or air-cooled mall cargo cult. In *Living For Less*, though, this hey presto is disrupted and graphically critiqued at an extremely subtle level; not about gadgetry or white goods any more.[1]

Having got her free catalogue, Toigo chose to print images of Michaelangelo's oil and tempera painting *Tondo Doni*, *c.*1506–7, onto its pages at regular intervals. A proto-Mannerist painting singular for having been carried out by Michaelangelo himself with no help from assistants (is Toigo drawing our attention to her own labours?), *Tondo Doni* is an image that divides art historians, who read it as either a devotional allegory or secular and domestic.

By means of precision cutting Toigo then skilfully effects a series of concentric circles progressively removing the book's content, and enabling the eye's giddy descent into a sinkhole, or *tondo*, where the original and overlaid blend into each other in an unstable fusion of high and low culture. Eventually, as if the rehearsed climax of a magician's stage act, an image of the holy family re-appears, resolved, despite the degradations it has suffered:

> "The Holy Family surrounded by toilet seats, Saint Joseph's head replaced by a watering can, Holy Mary pierced by cheap gold chains or the Baby used as a basketball by his careful parents are surreal and slightly heretical images."[2]

Perhaps having been exposed to *Living For Less*, anyone coming upon Michaelangelo's work during a visit to the Uffizi in Florence will now associate it with sports watches, food mixers and miscellaneous garden furniture!

---

1 *Det Gåtfulla Leendets Kavalkad*, 1964, was a 16mm film based on a mail order catalogue detourned by the Situationists Jørgen Nash, Sture Johannesson and Novi Marino.

2 lindatoigo.wordpress.com/2012/04/28/livingforless

The Master Plan

Stephen Hodge, 2012
—facsimiles, reconnaissance photographs

There is an unmistakable historical irony lurking in the title of Stephen Hodge's *The Master Plan*, which is on one level a straightforward collection of facsimiles of 58 typewritten, A4 Abermill Bond buff sheets: unpublished minutes transcribed from shorthand taken at an open meeting held between architects and the general public in Weston-super-Mare, 24 January 1947. The grand regenerative scheme presented with slides on this occasion by an architect from the practice of Mr Clough Williams-Ellis (renowned for designing Portmeirion, backdrop to the 1960s cult TV show *The Prisoner*) aimed at reconstructing the post-war resort, and was swiftly dubbed 'The Master Plan' by Weston's local press as if in sneering anti-authoritarian reference to the catastrophic downfall of Hitler's blonde Aryan heroes.[1]

The period deference and decency of the officials addressing the hall possesses a quaint charm:

> "I would like, before coming down to details, to utter one word of warning, or, rather, of consolation. By which I mean that you must not be frightened by this Plan. It is a long-term Plan. It does not mean that your house is going to be pulled down tomorrow, and turned into a public lavatory, or a shop, or an open space. We are trying to think 30 years ahead. It is a 30-year Plan."[2]

A member of the collective Wrights & Sites, Hodge was responsible for unearthing the original municipal folder labelled 'Town Planning —A/BWG/4/138pt1—1944—Post War Reconstruction', a discovery that would trigger off 'Everything you need to build a town is here', itself part of the über project *Wonders of Weston*, 2010. Hodge delineates how

> "Wrights & Sites use reconnaissance walking as a research method. The porosity of walking as a means of understanding place and the people you encounter is central to our practice."[3]

This methodology is expressed by 'annotations' juxtaposed beside the pages of the original document throughout *The Master Plan*: i.e. newspaper cuttings, vintage postcards, film stills, and quirky back street photographs; a compendious literary afterlife in dialogue with the unrealised 1947 proposal. Far from simplistically presenting a portrait of Weston as a failed utopia, though, the town emerges as an embattled site of multiple ongoing attempts to impose order and efficiency upon it, of ruins that never were, and as with all classic English seaside venues, amusement arcades, candy floss, donkey rides, guest houses and sanatoria, many staffed by low-paid seasonal workers; its tourist brochure promising sunshine, health and happiness while also being visited daily by one of the world's highest tidal rises, a lunar rhythm sometimes capable of generating a headline such as

> "Human Head and Bones found on beach."[4]

Hodge's artists' book has evolved crab-like from *matériel* retrieved in the archives of the North Somerset Studies Library, showing the versatility of a form that enables civic anamnesis, while acting as a limp covered holiday souvenir.

---

1 Indeed a model of the proposed Design for Weston does show a monumental development resembling the Nazi holiday destination of Prora, tagged in the TV documentary 'Jerry-Building: Unholy Relics of Nazi Germany', 1994, by the architectural critic Jonathan Meades as "…XXXL and then some".

2 See page 3 of the original transcript in Stephen Hodge, *The Master Plan* (London/Bristol: Book Works & Situations, 2012).

3 Ibid. See 'Afterword', Stephen Hodge in conversation with Claire Doherty.

4 *Weston & Somerset Mercury*, 30 September 2010.

Mémoires

Structures Portantes d'Asger Jorn

Guy Ernest Debord, Asger Jorn, (Permild & Rosengreen), 1959
—coarse sandpaper, offset [1]

It is generally accepted amongst neurobiologists that the silo theory of memory is inaccurate, memory being more a type of extremely complex and contingent reconstruction, a changing cartography of repeated yet slightly varied firing patterns in the hippocampus area of the brain, its neurons influenced through time by garnered impressions and beliefs. This uncommon model of memory, considering it a forward looking system of representations, or tool, was the one Debord and Jorn gravitated towards as if by instinct, in the joint production of *Mémoires*, and is declared by the book's unusual stylistics:

> "*Mémoires* is a radically antiproductivist work, or, more precisely an antiwork, whose discursive antiphonal form reflected the dérive's emphasis on collective play."[2]

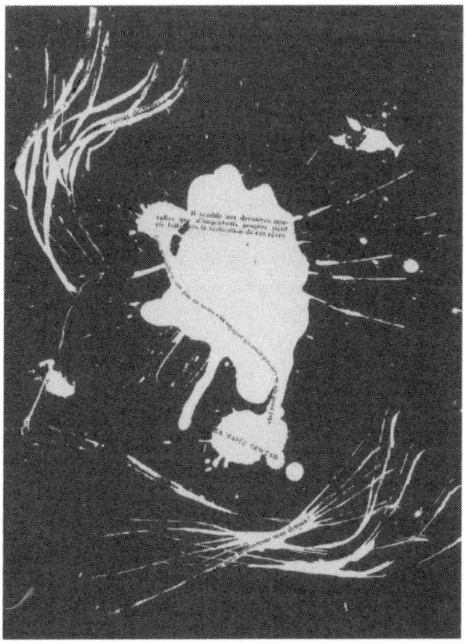

1959 saw Fidel Castro become premier of Cuba, the launch by Xerox of the first plain paper copier, and the extinction of the Caspian tiger; Walt Disney released *Sleeping Beauty* and the first direct dial payphones were introduced in the UK, but these are historically verifiable events, whereas Debord and Jorn's prefabricated scrapbook *Mémoires* (a lyrical tribute to their Parisian antecedents the Lettrist International) made of street plans, cut-out images of buildings, skewed textual odds and ends, and Rorsach-like tipped over colour washes has a fragmentary yet luscious look that graphically mimics the unconscious way the past is recalled and continually overlaid, as if Debord's strict parent were being undermined by Jorn's naughty boy flourishes.[3]

Held in thrall and continuous suspension by capitalist entertainment or conglomerated micro-spectacles, and a lifelong state of distraction and control, as a species we cannot even start the abreaction of painful conflicts, so wander amid fugues, forever lost, insatiable consumers. Psycho-analytically speaking, detourned material such as abounds in *Mémoires* becomes reconceived as evidence of therapeutic blockage, a symptom of this collective inability to retrieve traumatic memories; total recall or jouissance (perhaps symbolised by reference to Contrescarpe,[4] an arty hangout in the 5th *arrondissement*), a pipedream and Baudelarian ideal, though never entirely hors-de-texte. Set against this state of affairs the Situationist International's war cry[5] rings out, an arch ripple of antagonism towards neoliberalism's smooth hegemony.

Mémoires is paradoxically a speculative tool for navigating the megacity of tomorrow.

1 According to the printer this was "…to scratch neighbouring Morocco on the shelf or polished mahogany tables". www.christies.com/lotfinder/books-manuscripts/debord-guy-et-asger-jorn-5433945-details.aspx

2 Libero Andreotti, 'Architectural Play', in Tom McDonough (ed.), *Guy Debord and the Situationist International: Texts and Documents* (Cambridge, MA/London: MIT Press, 2002), p.217.

3 Between 1959 and 1962 Asger Jorn was engaged in the parallel activity of overpainting cheap pictures acquired from flea markets. His 'Modifications & Disfigurations' series included *The Disquieting Duck*, an early example of 'bad' art.

4 "Place de la Contrescarpe is the axis of a large, formerly working-class district, the ancient Faubourg Saint-Médard, gentrified, but still colorful, that spreads to the south on both sides of the market street Rue Mouffetard." www.writersinparis.com/formwritersinparis.php

5 Or 'Situ insults', as found in the detourned comic strip *Tout le Pouvoir aux Conseils Ouvriers! Les Syndicats ne sont qu'un Mécanisme d'Intégration á la Société Capitaliste! Les Travailleurs en Grève*. Published as a roneo by the S.I. in Paris circa late May or June 1968.

Murder Off Miami

Dennis Wheatley & J. G. Links, 1936
—facsimiles, samples, offset

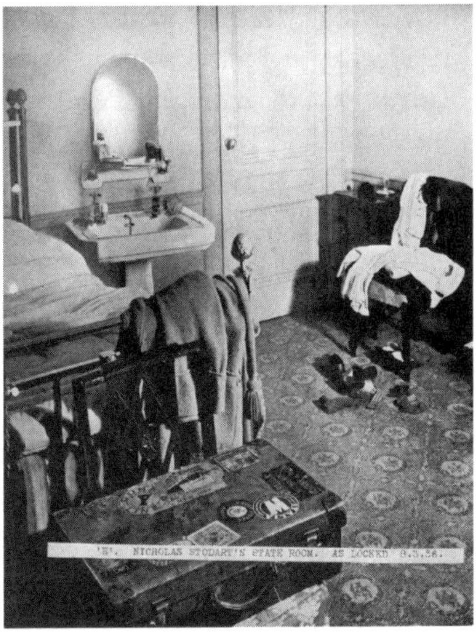

In *Murder Off Miami*, Messrs Wheatley & Links came up with the idea of an interactive crime mystery. Publisher Walter Hutchinson deserves credit for such a ploy, and facilitating the project for the Crime Book Society, London. By chance it is almost contemporaneous with Marcel Duchamp's *Green Box*, 1934, with its collection of 94 collotyped/pochoir notes pertaining to the mystery of Duchamp's own *The Bride Stripped Bare by her Bachelors, Even*, 1915–23, colloquially *The Large Glass*.

Murder Off Miami is a police dossier though, a quarto book with yapped soft covers bound by a red silk ribbon. It contains 138 pages of cablegrams, typescripts, police identification records, handwritten notes, both coloured and b&w photographic illustrations and plates. There are even several small sachets tipped in, for instance a used matchstick marked Adlon-Claridge, and some frank and sinister human hair described as being

> "Found in Miss Ferri Rocksavage's Comb on the Morning of 9.3.36.".

Handling a copy it is hard to resist the prosumerist temptation to undo its ribbon and disbind the pages of *Murder Off Miami*, which would doubtless complicate this 'whodunnit?' still further. The disordered outcome might quickly resemble the mayhem depicted in the forensic photograph of

> "Nicholas Stodart's State Room. As Locked 8.3.36.".

Nevertheless the urge to extend, elaborate and re-interpret is a testament to the pull of *Murder Off Miami*, in the same way that Richard

Hamilton expanded on Duchamp's medley of writings, contained in *The Green Box*, 1934.

In the 1950s pulp writer James Hadley Chase would compose fast-paced crime novels set in the USA, using street plans and maps of places he had never visited.[1] So in a sense they were conceptual in their basis, while more recently Roberto Bolaño has written dossier novels too, that appear empirical but are in fact complex confections, headaches to librarians unsure where to file such titles as *Nazi Literature in the Americas* (1996), that heavily conceals the author's own hand.[2]

Murder Off Miami does ask questions of the reader, not only challenging them to solve the mystery on the basis of the police evidence, but also ponder the types of writing presented here, where the novel has been rendered in document form.[3] Wheatley wants his fans to track down the killer via clues hidden in the dossier, but coming to terms with authorial intention is less interesting to an contemporary reader than appraising this display of many different linguistic codes and their relationships, an effect that cleverly blurs rather than suspends disbelief, whilst showing the indeterminacy of meaning, (especially in secondhand copies when the sealed strip containing the murderer's identity has invariably been opened and the answer lost!).

Murder Off Miami was subsequently reprinted many times as a conventional hardboiled paperback, but lacked the charm and off-beat format of the original, that places it if only unconsciously at the experimental fringes of the 20th century artists' book.

1 There is an echo of Arthur Conan Doyle here, as it is a popular misconception that Doyle knew London like the back of his hand, for as he himself admitted in an 1890 letter to the American publisher J. M. Stoddart, the first Holmes novel *A Study in Scarlet* (1888) had been worked out using a postal map.

2 Similarly the celebrated Spanish author and conceptual trickster Joan Fontcuberta, made up *Sputnik* (1997), a fable about a Soviet cosmonaut lost in space at the end of the Cold War. Consisting of fake photographs and other documentation Fontcuberta has admitted his "... satisfaction is when I find copies of this book in public libraries or universities, classified under the Russian History section or History of Aeronautics and not under Art or Fiction. The librarian who didn't pay enough attention, and his error gives these books a new life; they become time bombs waiting for an unsuspecting reader." 'A Bio-Optically Organised Knowledge Device Called 'Book'', Emmanuelle Waeckerlé & Richard Sawdon Smith (eds.), *The Book is Alive!* (2013), p.88.

3 Other period pastimes included Lassiter Wren & Randle McKay's *The Baffle Book* (Garden City, NY: Doubleday Doran & Co, 1928) described in *The Spectator* 29 November 1930, pp.29–33, as "...a refreshing substitute for crossword puzzles". Edgar Wallace's *The Crime Club Jigsaw Puzzle* (Long Island City, NY: Einson-Freeman Co, 1933), and Peter Cheyney's *The Crime Club Card Game* (London: Pepys/Castell Bros, 1935).

My Own Mag

Jeff Nuttall, 1963–66

—latrinalia, drawing, mimeo

Publisher Charles Boyle has asserted

> "…not untypically, a small gang of people who favour a branch of literature get something going."[1]

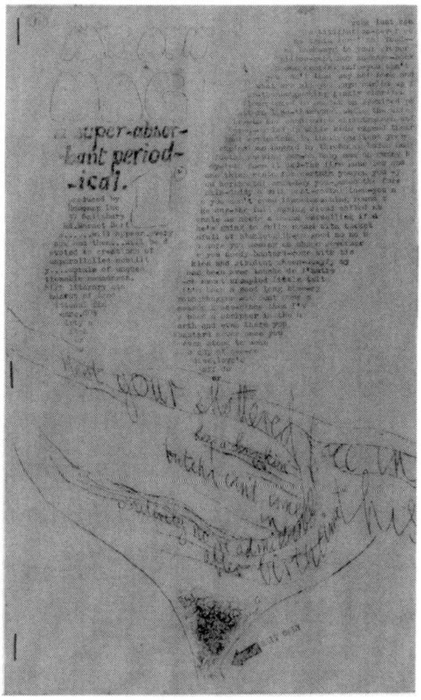

Besides creating a platform for his own scatological work, Jeff Nuttall invited a slew of writers and visual artists to contribute to *My Own Mag*, a ground-breaking 1960s zine.[2] The list included William S. Burroughs, Allen Ginsburg, Robert Creeley, Michael McClure, Alexander Trocchi, Anselm Hollo, Brian Patten, B. S. Johnson, Tom McGrath etc.

As a title, the emphatic possessiveness of *My Own Mag* flags up the new found freedom mimeography offered to its users, letting Nuttall and many others of that era experiment with home made publications by means of a Gestetner tabletop, side-stepping the deeply conservative Oxford/Cambridge literary nexus and Faber elite.[3] With the technical support of underground operative Bob Cobbing, *MOM* was printed off by hand. The process itself was of uncertain quality, with guaranteed blurs; though many a parish clerk doubtless became adept with the new technology:

> "The basic component of the duplicator was an ink-filled drum which was wrapped around a stencil, or 'skin'. The stencil was typed on and ink was forced through the cut letters, etc, on the stencil."[4]

Bibliographically speaking confusion reigns over the sequencing of all issues up to No.13 of *MOM*, (after which they became uniform) as they lacked 'straight' paratextual aids such as numbering and pagination.[5] But the subtitles of early editions of *MOM* such as

A Super Absorbant Periodical and *The Odour Fill Periodical* declared it was in sleaze mode from the outset, part of a revolutionary chain of small press production that has skipped from photocopy to desktop to today's e-zine. The significance of *MOM* lies elsewhere though, cathected in Nuttall's daring,[6] and the hospitality his zine offered to excluded writers. Collector Jed Birmingham has summed up the revolutionary legacy of *MOM* with aplomb:

> "To this day, the magazine has an aura about it, and it is a unique experience to flip through its pages. As book object and as content, *My Own Mag* captures the spirit of its time, yet remains fresh for today, and eerily relevant for the future."[7]

---

1 'Freelance', *Times Literary Supplement*, 7 February 2014.

2 realitystudio.org/bibliographic-bunker/my-own-mag/

3 "The possibilities of duplication (mimeographing) yawned invitingly. I turned out *My Own Mag: a Super-Absorbant Periodical* in November 1963 as an example of the sort of thing we might do. My intention was to make a paper exhibition in words, pages, spaces, holes, edges, and images which drew people in and forced a violent involvement with unalterable facts. The message was if you want to exist you must accept the flesh and the moment." Jeff Nuttall, *Bomb Culture* (London: MacGibbon & Kee, 1968), p.151.

4 Peter Hodgkiss, 'It's in the Garage…', Geraldine Monk (ed.), *Cusp: Recollections of Poetry in Transition* (Bristol: Shearsman Books, 2012), p.126.

5 More generally the lack of page numbers in artists' books allies them with early modern incunabula.

6 "I paint poems, sing sculptures, draw novels", *International Times*, no.9, 1967.

7 realitystudio.org/bibliographic-bunker/my-own-mag/my-own-mag-a-bibliographic-nightmare/

Naked Among the Clad

Vasilii Kamenskii, Andrei Kravtsov, 1914
—mixed media

Visually captivating and delectable, both *Naked Among the Clad* and its better known relative *Tango With Cows* (1914) are defined by their pentagonal shape: missing corners reminiscent of price clipped dust-jacket flaps. *NAC*'s crudely designed bedroom wallpaper shows variously a stag, boar, ox and vulture in red, violet and cold coffee tones, with *futuristy* Kamenskii's ferro-concrete poetry and Kravtsov's sketchy line drawings (allegedly) of vexed Bohemian figures lithographed on its reverse. Printed in an edition of 300, *Naked Among the Clad* belongs to a disruptive family of incendiary artists' books bearing earth shattering titles such as *A Trap for Judges* (1910), *A Slap in the Face of Public Taste* (1912), *A Game in Hell* (1912), *Worldbackwards* (1912), *Explodity* (1913) and *Roaring Parnassus* (1914).

> "Their homemade qualities communicate the idea that each volume is in some way unique, aimed at a coterie of friends."[1]

Indebted to Nietzsche, and an opponent of Pushkin, *fin-de-siècle* Symbolism as well as Marinetti's phonetic excesses, Kamenskii—who was jailed after his role in the 1905 revolution—also edited the *First Journal of Russian Futurists 1–2* (1914), holding ambitions to move way beyond books and inscribe poetry on fences, factory walls, airships, even the sky itself, and yet in *Naked Among the Clad* his tart verse prefigures Constructivism's sober typographics in its use of mixed fonts, grids, and distributed language, while also being somewhat indebted performatively to Wyndham Lewis's *Blast*.

> "The text is set within a geometric framework to resemble its namesake, the modern construction material of steel-reinforced concrete."[2]

This compartmentalising of stanzas, or segments, evokes variously Constantinople, nightclubs, a skating rink and a telephone but works best in his Shchukin Museum ground-plan poem for flâneurs:

> "The arrangement exactly follows the display of paintings in the museum, room by room. Kamenskii energetically involves his reader in a dialogue, an interaction, as if inviting him to come along."[3]

Both *Naked Among the Clad* and *Tango With Cows* belong to the end of the first exuberant phase of Russian Futurist bookware. Confronted by the double hiatus of the Great War and Bolshevik revolution, the neo-primitivist tendency of poets and artists such as Mayakovsky, the Burliuks, Kruchenykh and Khlebnikov would be tempered, as political necessity obliged them to march to a different drumbeat, one that aggressively declared the future to already be in town. For these figures, making small-format books had been a cacophonous rite expressed through their gleeful manipulation of archaic lettering, hand-drawn verse, and found documentation, which combined with material resources such as wallpaper and rubber stamps; fashioned artefacts that could be bought for anywhere between 30 and 70 kopeks.

Kamenskii's charming *zaumnik* verse with its dots, circles, columns and incomplete words laid down a significant modus operandi for what would come to be known as concrete poetry, a set of graphic tricks designed to

> "...put the world on a new axis".[4]

---

1 Deborah Wye, 'Art Issues/Book Issues: An Overview', in Margit Rowell, and Wye, Joanne Greenspun (ed.), *The Russian Avant-Garde Book 1910–1934* (2002), p.21.

2 Susan P. Compton, *The World Backwards: Russian Futurist Books 1912–16* (London: British Library, 1978), p.83.

3 Nina Gurianova, 'A Game in Hell, Hard work in Heaven: Deconstructing the Canon of Russian Futurist Books', *op. cit.*, p.30.

4 *41°*, newspaper, Tbilisi, 1919.

Observations

Relative Chiefly to Picturesque Beauty, Made in the Year 1772, on Several Parts of England; Particularly the Mountains, and Lakes of Cumberland, and Westmoreland.

William Gilpin, 1786
—aquatint, letterpress

Since the beginnings of their democratisation in the 18th century, the tourist/enthusiast armed with a box of watercolour paints, Claude Glass[1] and oilskin diary was an ambiguous figure, partly in search of uplifting sights and ennobling vistas, partly travelling abroad to expunge their crippling melancholy. For Gilpin, egged on by his friend the poet Thomas Gray to explore the Wye Valley, *Observations* was also used to test out aquatint technology on his readership.

> "The needle with thin lines in the distance and thicker ones in the background rendered very closely Gilpin's free strokes of the pen. Considerable variety of light, shade, and texture was conveyed by the aquatint, in some cases using as many as five tones on one plate."[2]

His legendary *Observations*, a term that became characteristic of a certain kind of travel literature produced as a result of journeys to therapeutic destinations such as the Wye Valley, Stowe Park or The Lake District, led to Gilpin being lampooned as Dr Syntax, a character in search of the picturesque invented by the comedian John Bannister, and further developed by the Georgian poet William Combe,

> "...a skin-and-bone hero, a pedantic old prig, in a shovel hat".[3]

Indeed Gilpin found himself constantly on the defensive, having to explain to a literal minded public, as well as opinionated academicians such as Joshua Reynolds, that his drawings were never intended to be seen as precise topographical likenesses, but sketches of picturesque ideas, unreliable fictions in other words.

> "As a drawer of existing scenes, you are held as the greatest of infidels. If a Voyager down the River Wye takes out your book, his very boatman cries out 'nay sir you may look in vain there'."[4]

But this absence of mimetic prissiness facilitated the sublime perspective, one completed by time alone:

> "Brecknock is a very romantic place, abounding with broken grounds, torrents, dismantled towers, and ruins of every kind."[5]

Sublime or ridiculous, Gilpin's 'tints'[6] became all the rage amongst the emerging leisured class, although today his medallions can appear little more than biscuit tin art.

---

1 Gilpin himself was not an aficionado of the Claude Glass, believing it prevented the natural training of the eye.

2 Carl Paul Barbier, *William Gilpin: His Drawings, Teaching and Theory of the Picturesque* (Oxford: Oxford University Press, 1963), p.71.

3 Joseph Grego (ed.), *Rowlandson the Caricaturist: A Selection from his Work with Anecdotal Descriptions of his Famous Caricatures and a Sketch of his Life, Times, and Contemporaries*, vol.II (Piccadilly, London: Chatto & Windus, 1880), p.248.

4 Letter, William Mason to William Gilpin, 8 January 1784.

5 *Observations*, p.51.

6 In the comic opera *The Lakers* (1797), Miss Veronica Beccabunga enthuses over the landskip between Derwent Water and Borrowdale, in effect using her picturesque tourist lenses in much the same way as a filter for a photographic app "I must throw a Gilpin tint over these magic scenes of beauty. (*Looks through the glass*). How gorgeously glowing! Now for the darker. (*Looks through the glass*). How gloomily glaring! Now the blue. (*Pretends to shiver cold*)."

Orange Rumba

Guy Begbie and family, 2012

— book, pyrotechnics, Latino dance music, head-mounted video camera

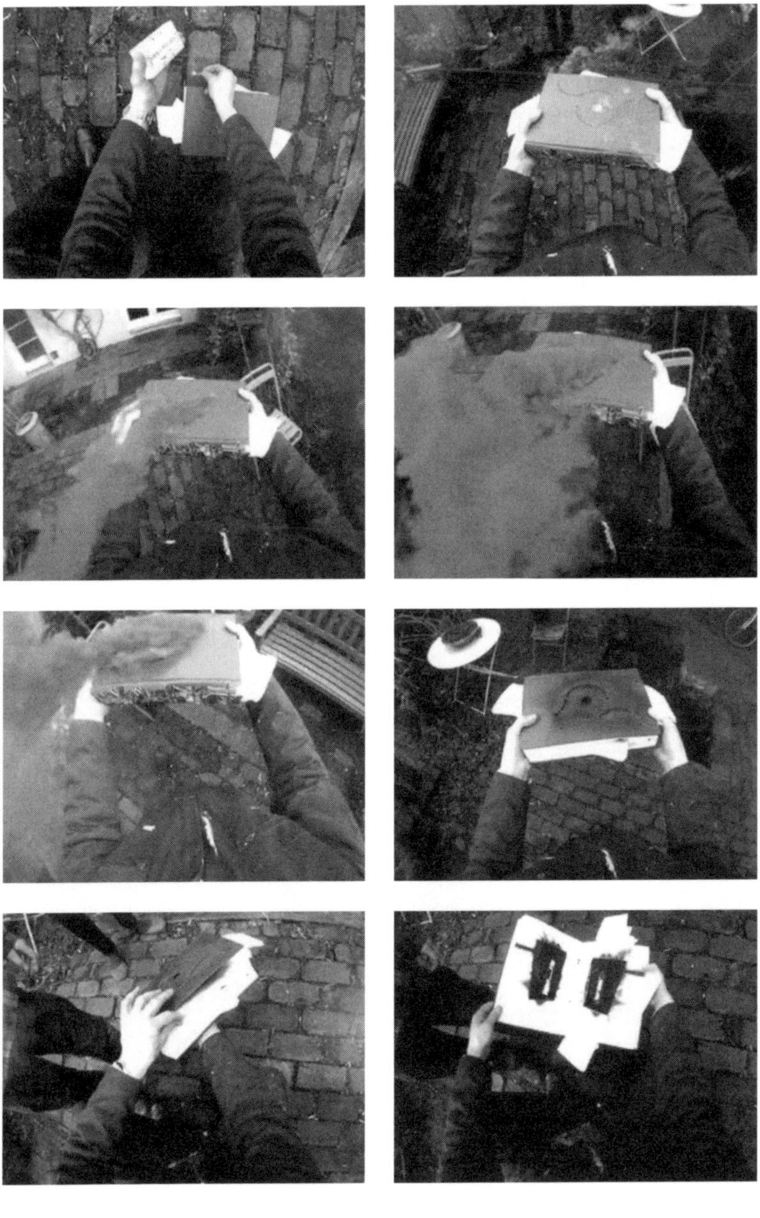

Guitar intro… household match… an extruded fuse… lit… to a bright and breezy rumba… silvery wisps of smoke… pale apricot signals… cue… hot brass section… orange smoke filtering through a perforated hardback… fuse channels… to a smuggler's cavity… *Statutory Instruments*… the sight is carnivalesque… full of glee… smoke pluming outward… abundantly… an active spin round 360 degrees… caught on headcam… as the rumba thickens… a blare of horns… crazed accordeon… a dry-as-dust book… transformed… host to a cockscomb of wayward orange smoke… doing its own Cuban dance… back yard antics… amongst push bikes and patio furniture… fabulous orange dye billowing… to leave a scorched impression… a hypocaust… of parliamentary legislation… *Statutory Instruments*… withdrawn… a Richter-like on-screen after blur… emancipation of the slaves…[1]

1 www.vimeo.com/37903577

LPDT2

Roy Ascott, 2010
—web project

An unjustly neglected figure in the history of 20th century art, Ascott's clunky neologisms 'telematic' and 'technoetics' have hardly become lingua franca, and so his pedagogic influence on students such as Pete Townshend, Brian Eno and Stephen Willats via his 'Groundcourse'[1] at Ealing Art College and later in Ipswich,[2] is oft-quoted, as if to compensate and cover up for a general lack of understanding and respect for Ascott's own work.

After a spell in radar control at the RAF, his sculpture from the late 1950s made from materials such as perspex, glass, wood, tin, baize, cellulose and aluminium situated him obliquely in the rarified English Constructivist camp, but with a theoretical overlay foreign to that milieu.

Roy Ascott went online for the first time in 1978! In 1983 his telematic project *La Plissure du Texte* was launched, intended to exemplify Roland Barthes concept of nonlinear narrativity and intertextuality, a planetary fairy story of dispersed authorship that created rewritable tissue-like texts through remote collaboration. Using ordinary computer terminals, keyboards connected to data projectors, a nodal weave linking mythical players from Amsterdam to Honolulu, Bristol to Pittsburgh and Vienna to Toronto was achieved via an I. P. Sharp timesharing global communication network.

Hank Bull who took part in *La Plissure du Texte* recalls how as data space

> "It was like a live radio or performance—that the value lay more in the event, the process, the shared experience of the project, than in the literary quality of the final outcome."[3]

The contemporary sequel *LPDT2* that allows public input via SMS

> "…seeks a new level of artistic creativity and technological expertise, dealing with distributed authorship in the metaverse of Second Life, involving textual mobility and the fluidity of an emergent poesis".[4]

Now the World Wide Web has normalised the multidisciplinary collaborations Ascott trailed for decades, finally validating his controversial initiatives to expand art education in unconventional, even wacky ways, and endorsing his futuristic approach.

---

1 For instance Ascott would get his students to draw the room in reverse perspective and then take note of what was lost in the process.

2 "We were set projects that we could not understand, criticized on bases that we did not even recognise as relevant." Brian Eno & Russell Mills, *More Dark than Shark* (London: Faber & Faber, 1986), p.40.

3 Email to Roy Ascott, 23 September 1998.

4 www.i-dat.org/roy-ascott-indaf-lpdt2syncretica/

Polygraphiae Libri Sex

Johannes Trithemius, 1518
—engraving, letterpress

As Benedictine Abbot of Sponheim Abbey, and erudite collector of a library of over 2000 religious, scientific and occult manuscripts and incunabula, Trithemius walked a dangerous metaphysical tightrope that could make him somewhat prickly, as in his dedicatory letter to the Emperor Maximilian that prefixes *Polygraphiae*,

> "I never engaged in intercourse with demons, in magic, necromancy, or study of profane arts. Who judges otherwise, judges wrongly."

However, he was intellectually curious, a Humanist attribute that opened the doors to modern times, a shifting double-dealer who believed in ceremonial magic, yet wrote three books against witchcraft.[1] In *De Laude Scriptorum* (1494) he declared himself steadfast in his opposition to the printing press, praising the virtues of parchment over paper.[2] Supremely confident in the divine truth of handwriting, Trithemius was disgraced after being found to have concocted false genealogies for the Hapsburg monarchy, falsified deeds to his own monastery to enhance its antiquity, and manipulated texts by Nicholas of Cusa among others!

Originally circulated in manuscript, his code-list and manual *Polygraphiae* is divided into books that form a system of alphabets, double-alphabets, word sets and nonsense or junk syllables with changing terminations as in a mill cipher. The text could be used to encrypt messages, and prevent information from being accessed by those without the key, also known as Kerckhoff's principle. Its *Ave Maria* cipher and square table encryption device remained in use for centuries.

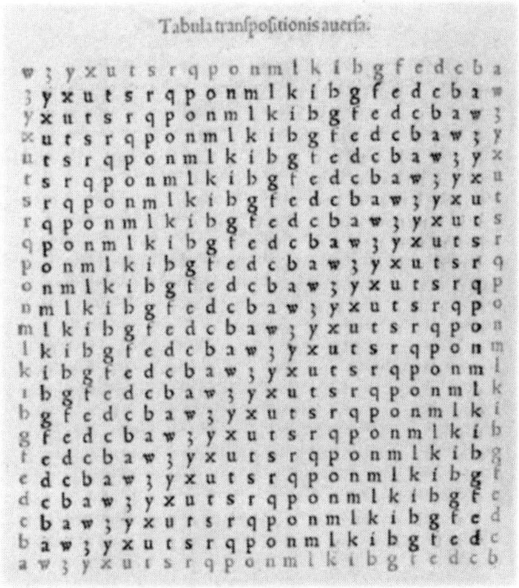

Tabula transpositionis aversa.

w	;	y	x	u	t	s	r	q	p	o	n	m	l	k	i	h	g	f	e	d	c	b	a
;	y	x	u	t	s	r	q	p	o	n	m	l	k	i	h	g	f	e	d	c	b	a	w
y	x	u	t	s	r	q	p	o	n	m	l	k	i	h	g	f	e	d	c	b	a	w	;
x	u	t	s	r	q	p	o	n	m	l	k	i	h	g	f	e	d	c	b	a	w	;	y
u	t	s	r	q	p	o	n	m	l	k	i	h	g	f	e	d	c	b	a	w	;	y	x
t	s	r	q	p	o	n	m	l	k	i	h	g	f	e	d	c	b	a	w	;	y	x	u
s	r	q	p	o	n	m	l	k	i	h	g	f	e	d	c	b	a	w	;	y	x	u	t
r	q	p	o	n	m	l	k	i	h	g	f	e	d	c	b	a	w	;	y	x	u	t	s
q	p	o	n	m	l	k	i	h	g	f	e	d	c	b	a	w	;	y	x	u	t	s	r
p	o	n	m	l	k	i	h	g	f	e	d	c	b	a	w	;	y	x	u	t	s	r	q
o	n	m	l	k	i	h	g	f	e	d	c	b	a	w	;	y	x	u	t	s	r	q	p
n	m	l	k	i	h	g	f	e	d	c	b	a	w	;	y	x	u	t	s	r	q	p	o
m	l	k	i	h	g	f	e	d	c	b	a	w	;	y	x	u	t	s	r	q	p	o	n
l	k	i	h	g	f	e	d	c	b	a	w	;	y	x	u	t	s	r	q	p	o	n	m
k	i	h	g	f	e	d	c	b	a	w	;	y	x	u	t	s	r	q	p	o	n	m	l
i	h	g	f	e	d	c	b	a	w	;	y	x	u	t	s	r	q	p	o	n	m	l	k
h	g	f	e	d	c	b	a	w	;	y	x	u	t	s	r	q	p	o	n	m	l	k	i
g	f	e	d	c	b	a	w	;	y	x	u	t	s	r	q	p	o	n	m	l	k	i	h
f	e	d	c	b	a	w	;	y	x	u	t	s	r	q	p	o	n	m	l	k	i	h	g
e	d	c	b	a	w	;	y	x	u	t	s	r	q	p	o	n	m	l	k	i	h	g	f
d	c	b	a	w	;	y	x	u	t	s	r	q	p	o	n	m	l	k	i	h	g	f	e
c	b	a	w	;	y	x	u	t	s	r	q	p	o	n	m	l	k	i	h	g	f	e	d
b	a	w	;	y	x	u	t	s	r	q	p	o	n	m	l	k	i	h	g	f	e	d	c
a	w	;	y	x	u	t	s	r	q	p	o	n	m	l	k	i	h	g	f	e	d	c	b

The first printed work on cryptography, *Polygraphiae* also bears some of the traits of the post-war artists' book, in so far as its meaning is opaque and methodology strange, at least to the uninitiated; while its value as a handbook led to its suppression by ecclesiastical authorities until the first printed edition at Basel in 1518.

The Norwich-based polymathic scholar Sir Thomas Browne owned a copy published at Cologne in 1571, and is credited with introducing the word 'cryptography' into the English language.

1 He compiled a bibliography for necromancers, *Antipalus Maleficiorum* (1605).

2 "Ironically, Tritheim's handwritten original of *In Praise of Scribes* has vanished, while 108 copies of his books, printed five hundred years ago on rag paper, sit on the shelves of North American Libraries." Hillel Schwartz, *The Culture of the Copy: Striking Likenesses and Unreasonable Facsimiles* (New York, NY: Zone Books, 1996) p.217.

Punched Cards for the Analytical Engine

Charles Babbage, 1837
—holed pasteboard

Derived from the operation cards of the Jacquard loom, whose complex hole arrangement determined any woven pattern, these were

> "...strung together with wire, ribbon on tape hinges, and fan-tailed into large stacks to form long sequences".[1]

Four classes of cards controlled both input and output to Babbage's Analytical Engine: Operational, Variable, Numerical and Combinatorial; outboard storage devices for the world's very first parallel processing digital computer, kept neat and tidy in an accordeon binding.

In the unlikely event of ever being separated from their museal context and thus their meaning as programming cards, this cache of Victorian artefacts might be examined and puzzled over with much difficulty, their actual function, if any, only to be guessed at: mute souvenirs of a lost civilisation perhaps, or part of a steampunk parlour game to which the rules have been lost?

Of course the supporting text at the Science Museum in London's Albertopolis district helps to establish the real purpose of these sturdy cardboard relics.

> "Working in conjunction with the barrels, the cards give instructions to the machine, from the start of the calculation to the printing out of the end result."

In an adjacent vitrine suspended in a jar simply labelled HOMO D685, is the right sagittal section with cerebellum of Mr Babbage's brain,[2] a specimen that since its dissection in 1907 has taken on a grubby cream/beige undercoat hue, bizarrely enough indiscernible in tone from the two little piles of punched cards that sit fading forlornly beside a full-size model of the legendary Analytical

Engine, precision engineering in all its brass glory which not unlike Babbage's bewitching technical drawings, viewable in an adjacent plan chest, radiates an intense, uncanny power.

A notorious perfectionist, Babbage was an oft frustrated entrepreneur who attempted to walk on water, drew up plans for a black box, and descended into Vesuvius to take readings. He also formulated a theory of miracles that made sense of untoward disasters by coding them as

> "...programmed discontinuities".[3]

---

1 Doron Swade, *The Cogwheel Brain: Charles Babbage and the Quest to Build the First Computer* (London: Little, Brown and Company, 2000), p.107.

2 Babbage's brain found itself temporarily imbricated with Dr Crippen's medicine chest, John Wesley's spurs and Florence Nightingale's writing slate, just some of the personal effects used by Cornelia Parker in her performance installation 'The Maybe', Serpentine Gallery, London W2, 4–10 September 1995.

3 *op. cit.*, p.79.

Reliquary Edge

Nigel Slight, 2012
—mixed media

Nigel Slight's work crosses disciplines, notably sculpture, installation, book arts, metagraphics and sound. He has freely confessed his failings as an old school draughtsman:

> "...drawing is the engine of praxis for the plastic arts, it is the working method that has been the most fluctuating and distracted in my work".[1]

Slight brings to bear, though, an investigative energy throughout his oeuvre, where uncertainty is fully embraced less as a style than an ontological precondition of making objects, a modality expressed in the unlikely physical outcomes of ready-to-use performance props such as *Treadplate Prayer Book* (nd).

Reliquary Edge was conceived for the group show 'Beneath the Covers', 2012, at Magg Bros antiquarian bookshop in London, with its remit to subvert craft. Ed Maggs describes how Slight

> "Considers the cultural preciosity of antiquarian books and documents, and the theme of human-initiated devastation."[2]

A conceit installed in the back garden, Slight recalls that his metamorphic piece

> "...was formed from 'cast' aluminium and thermal plastics attached to an adapted scaffolding sub structure. The aluminium 'cover/elevation' was made by pouring the molten metal onto a sheet of armour-plate glass, whilst the rear elevation/back cover formed from 25mm plastic sheet. The 'fore-edge/side elevation' is gilded and laminated sheeting

> of clear plastic. The spine/side elevation formed from sheet aluminium. The internal electrics, including hazard warning light and LED programmable signage bar are powered by transformed mains electricity. A page from the original prayer book can be viewed through a Fresnel lens set into the aluminium 'cover'. The electrics were on timer which lead to interesting developments in the local as the night drew in. The signage reads ...WORLD...WITHOUT...END...AMEN..."[3]

Edward's *Common Prayer* book, with its ornamental fore-edge,[4] duly sublimated.

---

1 www.fromfloortosky.org.uk/nigel_slight.html

2 www.maggs.com/book_collecting/maggs_journal/maggs-beneath-the-covers/

3 Email, 9 April 2014.

4 This fascinating practice consisted mainly of scrolls, fleurons and heraldic devices before the mid 18th century, when under the pervasive influence of William Gilpin's concept of the 'picturesque' formulated in *A Dialogue Upon the Gardens of the Right Honourable the Lord Viscount Cobham at Stowe in Buckinghamshire* (1748) book fore-edges often became the site for representations of arcadian scenes. Typically "...the motif only shows when the page is fanned out; when the book is closed straight, the painting disappears beneath a layer of gilding or marbling on the edges". www.kettererkunst.com/dict/fore-edge-painting.php

Rembrandt

Typex, 2013
—offset

Loosely based on a short story by Gert Jan Pos, Typex's *Rembrandt* depicts an inner city Rembrandt van Rijn, constituting a new warts-and-all graphic biography of the man:

> "Rembrandt's life, 1606–1669, spanned the height of the Golden Age, when the Netherlands was awash with bourgeois and aristocratic money, much of it spent on acquiring art, and the book is both sociological and historical."[1]

Opening with a strip of images that feature a startled elephant being winched ashore onto the quay side at Amsterdam from the darkness of a ship's hold, Raymond Koot aka Typex leads the reader through the rise and fall of Rembrandt, from his obscure beginnings as a lithe young provincial painter in Leiden, through to his sad end as a wordly wise, irascible old curmudgeon.

Rembrandt dwarfs all those who come into contact with him, overweight, dissipated and tetchy, his bulbous nose and dark eyes exert an influence over his immediate surroundings, be it tavern, studio, or street. Addicted to work, yet forever in search of patronage, he's often forced to cadge a drink or borrow funds to settle the rent with his overbearing landlady. This is a classic tale of Renaissance self-fashioning from below, stressing the painter's scheming roguishness.

Employing a muddy or clair obscur palette of ochre, raw sienna, bottle green, brick red and charcoal, Typex builds up a narrative from vignettes explicit in their energy and action. He cleverly varies his illustrative format, jumping around without regard for temporal continuity, sometimes eschewing speech bubbles entirely, and occasionally contrives marvellous close-ups of Rembrandt's brush applying a crude clot of paint onto stretched canvas.

A Rijksmuseum commission, and the result of three years labour, *Rembrandt* was published just as one of the old master's most famous paintings, *The Night Watch*, 1642, was moved back to the revamped museum.

At the end of this graphic novel darkness falls in Rembrandt's atelier, a gloomy interior bereft of his elephantine presence.

---

1 http://www.enca.com/life/new-light-rembrandts-darkness

Remember

People of Al-Mutanabbi Street

Bonnie Thompson Norman & Jill Alden Littlewood, 2013
— offset, burning, leatherette, gilt

After an explanatory text, all the recto pages in *Remember* contain the same list naming the 30 people killed by a huge car bomb detonated by unknown terrorists on 5 March, 2007, in Al-Mutanabbi Street (شارع المتنبي), Baghdad, each page uniquely distinguished only by the way posthumously their respective identities, age and profession have been removed through controlled burning, a process that has left behind a series of charred holes where once a person existed, uniting the dead regardless of their sectarian beliefs. This symbolic method of extinguishing them one by one re-enacts their utter obliteration, presenting an absence that cannot be repaired or filled, while sublimating their memory.

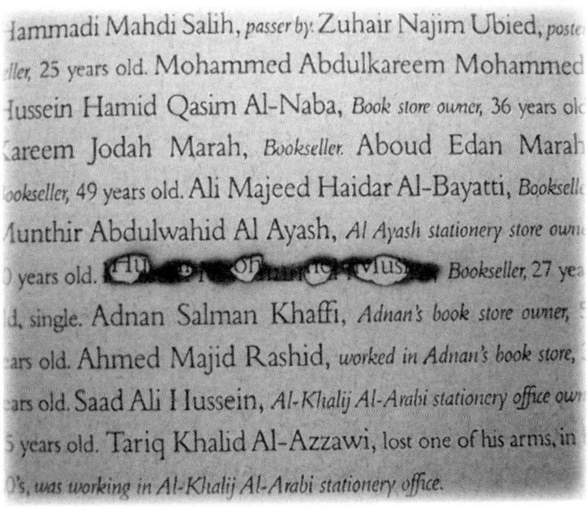
ammadi Mahdi Salih, *passer by.* Zuhair Najim Ubied, *poste*
ller, 25 years old. Mohammed Abdulkareem Mohammed
ussein Hamid Qasim Al-Naba, *Book store owner,* 36 years ol
areem Jodah Marah, *Bookseller.* Aboud Edan Marah
ookseller, 49 years old. Ali Majeed Haidar Al-Bayatti, *Booksell*
unthir Abdulwahid Al Ayash, *Al Ayash stationery store own*
years old. [illegible] *Bookseller,* 27 ye
d, single. Adnan Salman Khaffi, *Adnan's book store owner,*
ars old. Ahmed Majid Rashid, *worked in Adnan's book store,*
ars old. Saad Ali Hussein, *Al-Khalij Al-Arabi stationery office own*
years old. Tariq Khalid Al-Azzawi, lost one of his arms, in
'*s, was working in Al-Khalij Al-Arabi stationery office.*

On the verso pages, Saud Nass and his friend Faisal have written the lines in Arabic which translate as: *The memory of these people is in our hearts. Rest in peace.*

Remember is part of a growing efflorescence of broadsides, artists' books, posters and other ephemera that has been generated by the atrocity. 'Al-Mutanabbi Street Starts Here'[1] is a rhizomatic project and travelling archive instigated by Beau Beausoleil, proprietor of the Great Overland Book Company in San Francisco. Such a raft of deeply felt popular responses demonstrates the timeless power of literature, and just why the Baghdad book trade became a target of shadowy extremists: inherently seditious, the fusion of shop and café forms a classic commercial hub of intellectual revolution, and source of the unfettered exchange of ideas.

> "One link in this circulation process, for example, is the bookstore, one of the primary means for the movement of published marxist, critical and progressive theory."[2]

In 2009, Jeremy Deller and friends headed off on a marathon road trip from New York to Los Angeles in a specially outfitted RV, pulling the mangled remains of a car caught in the Al-Mutanabbi blast on a trailer; a mobile talking point wherever it halted. Interviewed by Deller, Esam Pasha, an Iraqi citizen travelling aboard, who worked as an interpreter for the US 101st Airborne Division in his homeland, summed up what the thoroughfare meant for him:

> "Al-Mutanabbi Street was the informal cultural center of Baghdad, it was where intellectuals and artists gathered to discuss ideas and exchange information. Every city needs a place like this. Art galleries and an auction house joined booksellers along the street. During the embargo, people sold their own books, becoming book dealers by default. It happened to me. People would approach you and ask you to sell their library for them. Professional sellers were there all week, and they would find or photocopy books for you. The street was a refuge or sanctuary, and also a place to find about cultural events. The Shabandar Café was the heart of the street."[3]

The wreckage from Deller's project 'It Is What It Is'[4] was donated to the Imperial War Museum in 2010.

---

1 www.al-mutanabbistreetstartshere-boston.com

2 Seth Siegelaub, 'A Communication on Communication', in Armand Mattelart & Seth Siegelaub (eds.), *Communication and Class Struggle: An Anthology in 2 Volumes. 1: Capitalism, Imperialism* (New York/Bagnolet: International General, 1979), p.16.

3 Jeremy Deller, *It Is What It Is* (New York: Creative Time Books, 2010), p.5.

4 www.conversationsaboutiraq.com/description.php

Sapolio soap volvelle

Enoch Morgan's Sons Co., 1940s
—cardboard, grommet, letterpress

According to Michael Ryan, it is a lamentable state of affairs that

> "For too long we have chosen to identify printed matter that does not neatly fit our categories of cataloging and description as 'ephemera',[1] that is material that is transitory by design and thus neither intrinsically important nor worth the labor of cataloging."[2]

Variously known as slide or wheel charts, information discs, rotational diagrams or spinners, volvelles—despite being terribly under-appreciated and regarded as anachronistic vestiges from the last days of the Ptolemaic universe—were probably introduced into the west by Raymond Lull, and actually offer according to Ryan

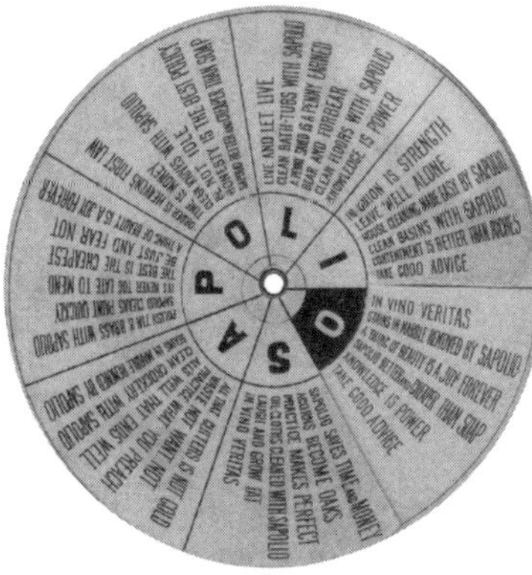

> "...everything from inventory control to color calibration, mileage metering to verb conjugation. They anticipate animal breeding cycles and calculate radiation exposure, measure chocolate consumption and quantify bridge tips, chart bird calls, convert metrics and calculate taxes. They are fortune-telling wheels; emergency first-aid wheels and electronic fix-it wheels; playful wheels that test phonetics and prophylactic wheels that prevent pregnancy".[3]

It might have been added that sometimes these discs turn up attached to book marks with line and column indicators, as in the one tucked inside a 13th century bible from St Augustine's Abbey, Canterbury, England, or as astrological appendices such as the paper wheel cut out and sewn into an almanac, *Parker's Ephemeris for the Year of Our Lord 1710* belonging to the Folger library.[4]

Trapped disc volvelles that can aid financial investment, sales training, or even colour code visualisation, sit uneasily between kinetic thinking and the logic of the modernist grid.

---

1 A leaflet (nd) promoting the Bodleian Library's John Johnson Collection of printed ephemera, defines it as "...material which was not intended to survive its immediate purpose".

2 Michael Ryan, 'Helfand, Jessica, *Reinventing the Wheel: Volvelles, Equatoria, Planispheres, Fact-Finders, Gestational Charts...* (2002)', *College & Research Libraries*, vol.64, no.1, January 2003, p.93.

3 Ibid.

4 Brooke S. Palmieri notes on her blog that "Based on its ability to yield calculations, however simple, the volvelle is considered an early example of a computer. But you can also find one that doesn't compute anything on the album sleeve of *Led Zeppelin III*." www.eightvo.wordpress.com/2012/06/25/an-introduction-to-paper-computers/

Sepulchral Monuments in Great Britain

Applied to Illustrate the History of Families, Manners, Habits, and Art, at the Different Periods from the Norman Conquest to the Seventeenth Century with Introductory Observations

Richard Gough, 1786–96

—engraving, fold-out pedigrees, letterpress

Bibliographic hypertrophism is rife both in the prolixity of their title, the paving slab size of these two volumes, (cf. G. H. Pertz's forbidding *Monumenta Germaniae Historica* (1826), George Ormerod's burly History of Cheshire, or James Douglas's overlooked *Nenia Britannica* (1793) that carry a distinct risk of herniation to users), and lastly retail price (the complete Gough set cost twenty-one guineas new, or approximately £1400 today).

Dedicated to tracing the misty links between romanticism and archaeology, the art historian Kenneth Clark referred to Gough's monumental tome as one that can

> "...conjure up for us the tallest and dustiest shelves in a library".[1]

The two volumes in Humanities 1 Reading Room at the British Library are on open shelves, making them accessible to all registered users, in contrast to their original readership, of whom Clark remarks

> "These books usually contain a list of subscribers, which shows that they appealed to the leisured and aristocratic; and we might assume that before 1800 the taste for Gothic archaeology was confined to a small clique."[2]

Though the craze for sham ruins, disputes over the definition of Gothic and likewise attacks on contemporary restoration methods had been raging since the 1780s, it was kickstarted proper as a waspish paper war by a reprint in 1800 of four essays on the history of Gothic architecture by Messrs Warton, Bentham, Grose and Milner. Richard Gough himself was a hands-on antiquarian who carried a swish-whip, and spent twenty years touring the country in pursuit of the 'strang', more interested in learning for its own sake than the Walpolean faction within the Society of Antiquaries, who promoted taste. A prolific writer of articles for *The Gentleman's Magazine*, he wrote up his fieldwork in the library at Gough Park, Enfield, a space equipped with

> "...a chimney piece depicting Minerva putting giants to flight, originally from the house at Theobalds Park, while on each side of the chimney-breast were monumental brasses. All manner of curiosities were to be found in this room, a Roman satyr from Castor, vying with Indian idols, Chinese bronzes, inscriptions from many countries, a cast of a bronze head of Apollo found at Bath, Indian bows, arrows and lances."[3]

Richard Gough died in 1809 after a series of *grand mal* convulsions.

---

1 Kenneth Clark, *The Gothic Revival: A Study in the History of Taste* (London: Constable, 1950), pp.95–96.

2 Ibid., p.96.

3 Philip Whittemore & Chris Byrom, *A Very British Antiquary: Richard Gough 1735–1809* (London: Wynchmore Books, 2009), p.29.

Sheila Hicks

Weaving As Metaphor

Edited by Nina Stritzler-Levine, 2006

—textile reproductions, offset [1]

Touted in superlative terms since winning a medal at the Leipzig Book Fair in 2006, *Weaving*[2] is certainly a de-luxe publication, a marvel guaranteed to enrich the senses of any reader who comes into contact with what was adjudged

> "...the most beautiful book in the world".

At first glance, *Weaving* appears in the guise of a white box, roughly cut, deckle edges flush with the cover boards reminiscent of boutique hotel towelling. Inside, the font of a short essay by Arthur Danto (that refreshes the significance of weaving as political metaphor via Plato's *The Statesman*) gradually decreases in point size before the exhibition catalogue starts *per se*.

In her long career Hicks, who calls her smaller textile work 'minimes', has deployed wool, silk, shoelaces, bast, crumpled paper, razor clam shells, rubber bands and stainless steel fibre to produce hundreds of colourful selvedged swatches, which on average measure 10 x 5 inches, and resemble chain mail pages, the logical consequence of the daybooks she has kept since the late 1950s, sketching the sights and sounds of her peripatetic life. Their titles alone are exotic, i.e. *Zapallar*, Chile, 1957, or *Roulade Amazone*, Paris, 1965. *Back from the Front*, Jerusalem, *c*.1979, is a stitched marvel, an enhanced readymade:

> "Khaki green T-shirt is repeatedly sewn with a sharp needle."

Tutored by Bauhaus colour theorist Josef Albers while at Yale from 1954–59, and advised by his wife Anni to investigate pre-Columbian art, Hicks lived through an era that saw textiles leave the wall and emerge as an international 3D art form in their own right, concept and material inextricably woven together. Even so, for Seth Sigelaub, who as a conceptually biased gallerist[3] in the 1960s exhibited the rugs and textiles he collected, building up a complementary bibliography of books and a database[4] on the subject, was a smart way to get textiles taken still more seriously, since as Sara Martinetti notes

> "...we see that the bibliography and the loom are two systems that allow the concatenation of individual elements. Applied in one work after the other, page after page, the rules of bibliographic invention, like the weaving of threads, constitute lists as long as a roll of cloth."[5]

1 'Sheila Hicks: Weaving as Metaphor', The Bard Graduate Center for Studies in the Decorative Arts, Design and Culture, New York, 12 July–15 October 2006.

2 A video of book designer Irma Boom talking about the project can be seen at www.vimeo.com/703587

3 Seth Siegelaub Contemporary Art was located at 56th Street New York, and ran from 1964 to 1966.

4 www.egressfoundation.net

5 Sarah Martinetti, 'Seth Siegelaub and the Commerce of Thoughts', in the catalogue to 'The Stuff that Matters', Raven Row, London E1, 1 March–6 May 2012, p.38.

Spring Snow – A Translation

Alison Turnbull, 2002
—colour swatches, offset

Book Works' self-contained jacket blurb informs its readership that

> "Drawing on Mishima's evocative use of colour in the novel, Alison Turnbull condenses the narrative into a colour chart. Working from the English edition, she isolates and orders each of the more than six hundred colours as they appear in the text—what emerges is a visual essay on the nature of translation."

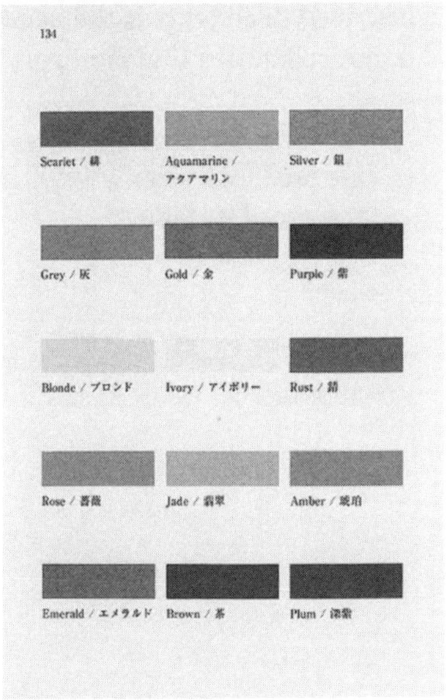

Namely: sepia yellow white red violet blue black crimson green scarlet aquamarine silver grey gold purple blonde ivory rust rose jade amber emerald brown plum indigo pink coral khaki azure orange bronze maroon russet magnolia ashen.

Spring Snow (1969) was the first novel in Yukio Mishima's tetralogy 'The Sea of Fertility', and charts a fatal love affair played out against the social backcloth of new money's tectonic effect on an ancient imperial order.

Less translation than quasi-Oulipean chromatic extraction and *ekphrasis*, Turnbull's rendition acknowledges the heavy phenomenological freighting of the source text, her translation conveying the tale with austere charm:

> "An old war photograph, a cloth falling off of a table, the way light plays over the face of a waterfall, etc, Mishima is able to forge rich emotional states around such images and to make them react and magnify each other."[1]

Turnbull's inventory and re-decorated narrative that obsessively tracks colour through the text is the kind of non-literary exercise that would have been approved of by Vladimir Nabokov, whose *Lectures on Literature* (1980) contained an appendix dedicated to sample exam questions, such as 'No.21: Follow Mr Guppy through *Bleak House*'. *The Nabokov Paper* (2013) took up this baton, inviting a group of writers and visual artists to respond to a fictional exam paper. Forbes Morlock indexed the horses in *Mansfield Park*, Guillaume Constantin graded the characters in *Bleak House* according to their shadow colour, while Christian Bök graphed *The Strange Case of Dr Jekyll and Mr Hyde* through the frequency with which the two names occur both by chapter and *passim* (199 times), noting how

> "The diagrams thus abbreviate the plot, depicting it as a fluctuation in the rise and fall of 'characters'—both as persons and as letters themselves."

Such an identification and re-coding of the repressed contents inscribed in all texts is the wand of active intelligence, a trade in unnoticed quirks that confirms their virile afterlife as 'classics', since

> "Translations that are more than the transmissions of a message are produced when a work, in its continuing life, has reached the age of its fame."[2]

1 www.goodreads.com/book/show/62793.Spring_Snow

2 Steven Rendell, 'The Translator's Task', *Traduction, Terminologie, Rédaction*, vol.10, no.2, 1997, p.154.

SW4 OHY

Vito Drago, 2002
—carved book, franked stamp

A slightly chilling anthropological snapshot, scraped off the internet as background to Vito Drago's modified book *SW4 OHY*, profiles the culture of a single street, in this case The Pavement, Clapham, London:

> "*Area: SW4 0HY. Area Type: Affluent Singles & Couples in Exclusive Urban Neighbourhoods.* Located in fashionable city and suburban areas, these affluent neighbourhoods are characterised by pre and post-family couples and singles. These residents live in small but expensive flats and terraces which they typically rent or mortgage, although some are wholly owned. Highly qualified, they represent the highest proportion of company directors in the UK. Others are employed in professional and white collar occupations in the service, IT and financial sectors. They frequently use the internet and read the quality press. They are active investors with a lower than average credit risk."[1]

The impersonal tone emphasises that the information is less about the well-being of the people and more to do with their spending power, above all creditworthiness. It is a fair bet Drago would be uninterested in such postcode research, but the piece is a kind of relic spent from his time living locally, and belongs to the 'LDN' series of books referencing London streets. In *SW4 OHY* the carved out map comes minus street names, although again further time spent with an A–Z quickly allows an empirical correlation to be made.

Drago's mixed-media, book-based sculptures variously feature deletion, letter transfer and evisceration, the tearing away of all bibliographic value in short, that irrevocably finishes the systemic withdrawal of any volume he has chosen to change; leaving them unreadable. The channels carefully cut into the pages of *SW4 OHY*, for instance, resemble blind alleys for a drugged-up lab animal to scurry down. Such manipulations express an anarchic contempt for the codex as ancient container of knowledge, the target of a Socratic zero sum game. In the cognate work *Which Direction ii (24/7)* (2005), a yellow-and-black surveillance camera sticker draws us into his paranoia too.

Drago has said of his work that

> "…I do not intend to define this city, but rather allude to its morphology."[2]

Yet his book works are full of gravitas, and have been eulogised by blogger Marina Faggioli:

> "Hanno qualcosa di funero, le opere di Vito Drago. Sono i forni di un cimitero dei libri, strade pieni do solitudine dove si viene spiati da telecamere silenti, il tracciato che presumibilmente registra una morte."[3]

1 www.192.com/places/sw/sw4-0/sw4-0hy/

2 www.englandgallery.com/artist_bio.php?mainId=63

3 "They have something of the funereal, the works of Vito Drago: ovens of a book cemetery, streets full of solitude watched by silent CCTV, a passageway where death must be registered." www.tuttalacartadelmondo.blogspot.co.uk/2009/11/vito-drago.html

Twentysix Gasoline Stations

Ed Ruscha, 1963
—photographs, offset

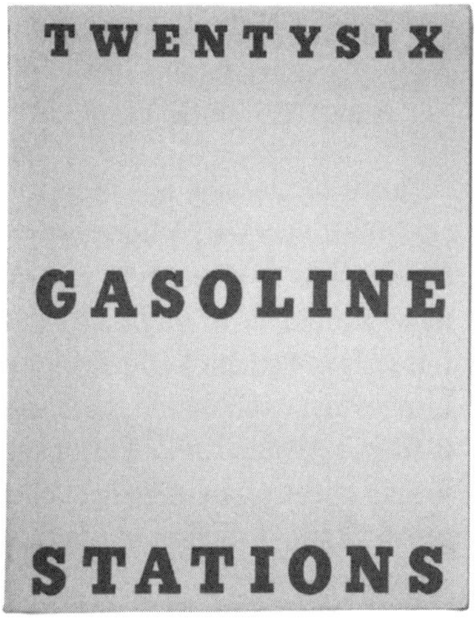

Ed Ruscha's work is filled with representations of parking lots, real estate, swimming pools, Hollywood signage and palm trees, though he is probably still best known for his mordant collection of photographs, *Twentysix Gasoline Stations*. His eye, and predilection for such Americana, seems to have been clearly focused after a youthful road trip along Route 66 from Oklahoma City to LA, made with guitarist buddy Manon Williams.[1] Citing this event, Michael Auping has remarked that

> "...experiencing the American West from the windshield of a car is to come close to understanding Ruscha's peripatetic vision of the world".[2]

Less *nature morte* than *architecture morte*, the deadpan photographing of vernacular sites has since become a highly influential mode, a complete toning down of the Gothic sublime in terms of choice of lens, specific material, and above all form (i.e. a non-hierarchical documenting practice accesible to all in the pages of a cheap self-published book), from which a wry postmodern scenography has emerged.

Even though a great deal of ink has already been wasted on *Twentysix Gasoline Stations*, here is a little back story concerning its reception.

> "For a period of a couple of years in the mid-1960s, when *Artforum* was based in Los Angeles, the magazine's offices were in the same building as Ed Ruscha's studio. Ruscha, who had trained as a commercial artist, occasionally did layout and design work for the magazine (appearing on the masthead under the name 'Eddie Russia'). *Artforum*, in those days, was

perpetually on the brink of financial insolvency and so, in the March, 1964 issue, Ruscha took advertising space in lieu of payment and used it to promote *Twentysix Gasoline Stations*, the first of his celebrated publications. The ad offers the book for $3 a copy. Upon publication Ruscha had sent a copy for inclusion in the Library of Congress's collection, but the librarian who had reviewed the submission was, apparently, nonplussed and declined to accept it. The book was returned to Ruscha without explanation. Ruscha turned this into a selling point, touting its 'REJECTED' status in this ad."[3]

This is proverbial, and indicative of the historical struggle for acceptance waged by book artists, one that has taken place at the margins of visual culture. Less a case of rejection in fact and more a moment of snobbish exclusion, and institutional disavowal not only of Ruscha's affectless subject matter but also his lack of intellectual explanation, paratextual aid or even a story.[4] However it is from between the cracks of such dumb concrete that the vibrant weeds of the modern artists' book genre grew and has continued to grow, gaining traction in the face of widespread and often hostile incomprehension.

Nevertheless, despite the well circulated bromide that *Twentysix Gasoline Stations* constitutes ground zero for the artists' book, and its timely appearance an austere apotropaic charm against the messiness of Abstract Expressionism,[5] *Twentysix Gasoline Stations* was only a nodal point in a far larger network of family resemblances, one still being uncovered and redesignated right now.

1 Appropriately, Williams went on to have a 1968 pop hit with *Classical Gas*.

2 Michael Auping, 'A Long Drive', p.11, in the catalogue to 'Ed Ruscha: Road Tested', Modern Art Museum of Fort Worth, Texas, 23 January–17 April 2011.

3 Johan Kugelberg and Jeremy Sanders, *Artists' Books Not Artists' Books* (2012).

4 "His witholding, erasure, or dislocation of text and information can be read as melancholic critical reflections on the erosion of cultural memory." Meghan Dailey, 'Hot Type: Ruscha on the Book', *Modern Painters*, April 2013.

5 Although Ruscha has actually got his hands dirty from time to time. See his portfolio 'Stains', 1969, that used gunpowder, chocolate syrup, bourbon and human blood.

Urbanomic

@urbanomicdotcom, 2010–
—*Twitter account*

A live feed and extensive archive of tweets and re-tweets (standing at 4,684 on 23 June 2015), the ongoing handiwork of Robin Mackay, director of Urbanomic, a publisher and arts organisation based at The Old Lemonade Factory, Falmouth:

> "...aiming to engender interdisciplinary thinking and production".

The strapline is fully endorsed by Urbanomic's own house journal *Collapse: Journal of Philosophical Research and Development* and its back catalogue of titles such as *Hydroplutonic Kernow* (2015), and François Laruelle's *From Decision to Heresy: Experiments in Non-Standard Thought* (2012), although a cognitive focus is sometimes hard to discern. No matter.

Tweeting as a pastime and market-driven messaging activity or imposture has overtaken Wordpress blogging, the ultra-disposable 140 characters a distinct sign of having less time to spare, with the need to compact more data as a result. Urbanomic's addition to the drone of inconsequential free-range information is an entertainingly mixed bag such as consumer/clinical mental health updates after overdoing Starbuck's Frappuccino, a link to a close-up image of the ingredients in a can of fizzy Black Grape (45% sugar) mashed up with diverse pop philosophy references to Accelerationism, Folk Politics, Object-Oriented Philosophy, Speculative Realism, Nordic noir, the shoot'em up scene at the Guggenheim Museum in the film *The International* (2009), so-called forensic 'Yarnwork' and rats.

This is an unstuffy way for a publisher to carry on, industrious too (we learn from a tweet dated 16 March 2015 that Mackay has 449 emails to reply to before "starting work"!), but not so far from the roguish promotional antics of 18th century stationers such as John Dunton and Edmund Curll, unregulated, frontier-like behaviour, where transgressive personality is an avatar that bleeds into the short-form narrative.

Immediacy typifies the medium, immateriality haunts its heart. Lyrical rather than logical, yet terrific as a trade notice board for the latest commercial news (a tweet dated 12 June 2015 plugs the release of Laboria Cubonik's *Xenofeminism: A Politics for Alienation*), Twitter represents a unique way for the modern publisher to attempt to reach their potential audience, and build a following; one moreover who might buy the books.

Reading through Urbanomic's vertical archive of messages it starts to become clear that this meta-publication can legitimately be seen as a species of artists' book in itself, one loosely bound by the internet, and no longer subconsciously copy-fitted to the old-fashioned printed page.

Webster Withdrawn

Brian Dettmer, 2010
—sculpted encyclopaedia

Brian Dettmer's working methods are determined by self-imposed constraints resulting in complex layered sculptures or dioramas that emerge from the interior of a physical book (generally redundant or outmoded reference volumes). Initially sealed, the books he selects to cut and carve into, or collaborate with, will have nothing new added, nor any contents shifted around. This is excision, textual clearance in which, however, chance is allowed a say, Dettmer's habitual means of exposure a cross between miniature stage-set design, and the industrial hard graft and know-how of a tiny building site. His hands-on modifications fuse the glassy-eyed intensity of a Richard Dadd painting with the precision engineering of a Hornby 00 gauge model railway set, intricate samples mobilised to prove his thesis that

> "The age of information in physical form is waning. As intangible routes thrive with quicker fluidity, material and history are being lost, slipping and eroding into the ether. Newer media swiftly flips forms, unrestricted by the weight of material and the responsibility of history. In the tangible world we are left with a frozen material but in the intangible world we may be left with nothing. History is lost as formats change from physical stability to digital distress."[1]

Webster Withdrawn, as the titles declares with tongue firmly in cheek, is no longer part of a library reference system, coming very much from the artisanal wing of the artists' book phenomenon which itself has become a significant locus for a broader re-skilling narrative, a *gemütlich* reaction to the perceived laziness of much nominative conceptual art, or the catachresis of bad art in general. And yet a slight air of craft masonry clings to Dettmer's excavations.

Also active in this very time consuming mode, the Bristol-based Berliner Alexander Korzer-Robinson has a liking for defunct books such as French Larousses, *Boy's Own Annual* or edifying religious literature that end up exquisitely cut out, as if he and Dettmer were illustrating the very idea of illustration itself. He notes how

> "...eventually a new story develops of its own volition".[2]

It says a lot for changing attitudes that such razor-sharp interventions are seen today as mainly symbolic of the erosion of knowledge, while the controversy that surrounded the physical destruction of books has largely been quelled. Founder of Reverb Technologies, lexicographer Erin McKean, recommends their online dictionary Wordnik

> "...which aggregates more than just word meanings: it includes context of the word, including usage and from Project Gutenberg and Wikipedia, Twitter feeds and Flickr photos that include the word being looked up, and also allows users to add their own meaning and context to the words".[3]

This is revolutionary in terms of access, epistemology and prosthetic use in a way Dr Johnson could never have dreamed of as he staggered round with his own two-volume dictionary inside his "Patagonian pockets".[4] Like it or not there can be no *rappel à l'ordre*.

1 www.laurencesternetrust.org.uk/exhibition.php?id=176

2 www.liberty-gallery.com/exhibiting-artists/508986_alexander-korser-robinson-.html

3 www.washingtonpost.com/wp-dyn/content/article/2009/07/08/AR2009070802728.html

4 'Peter Pindar', real name John Wolcot, in *Johnsoniana; or, Supplement to Boswell* (London: John Murray, 1836), p.xix.

York Tablets

Anon, 14th century
—boxwood, black wax, slip-case

This archaeological find is a splendid example of a 'girdle book', a type of primitive Filofax. Found during an archaeological excavation at Back Swinegate, York, in 1989

> "…which, in the medieval period, was occupied by dwellings and small craft workshops; in a patch of muddy wasteland a dark brown rectangular waterlogged object was spotted".[1]

It represented a major conservation challenge, which involved x-raying, computer tomography, followed by the separation of the eight waterlogged, fused-together tablets using Melinex® (a thin polyester sheet), stabilisation of the boxwood and preservation of the wax by means of freeze drying, and lastly consolidation of the tablets, recessed on both sides with a methyl cellulose-based polymer.

The case appears to hold three discrete texts: a bawdy lyric in a ridge-and-furrow script known as *cursiva anglicana* that has yet to be fully transcribed, a set of columnar accounts, and a portion of a legal document written in Latin, plus what appears to be a dumb-bell shaped ownership mark. Michelle P. Brown has remarked that

> "This intimate little object undoubtedly plays an important part in our assessment of the role of the wax tablet and of late medieval literacy."[2]

Unfortunately the girdle book's iron stylus that would have been used to incise marks on the wax sheets was very badly corroded, so this pen's disintegration along with the necessary if highly museumistic embalming of the messages complicate, indeed deny, the intrinsically unstable nature of such writing, viz the Mystic Writing Pad, a gizmo that fascinated Freud, who thought the psyche had a perceptual surface that acted as a sheath to the unconscious,

> "On the Mystic Pad the writing vanishes every time the close contact is broken between the paper which receives the stimulus and the wax slab which preserves the impression."[3]

The Snoopy Mini Memo Wipe Board, and Etch A Sketch[4] were both direct descendants, the latter a lineographic toy with horizontal and vertical knobs, which became popular in the 1960s and '70s. Deletion involved turning the screen over and shaking it.

It is most unlikely that the identity of the notebook's owner, dropped by accident in a York tenement yard around six hundred years ago, will ever be discovered.

---

1 www.yorkarchaeology.co.uk

2 Michelle P. Brown, 'The Role of the Wax tablet in Medieval Literacy: a Reconsideration in Light of a Recent Find from York', *The British Library Journal*, vol.20, no.1, spring 1994, p.13. Open Access Rare Books 027.541

3 'Notiz Uber Den 'Wunderblock'', James Strachey (ed.), *The Standard Edition of the Complete Psychological Works of Sigmund Freud* vol.XIX, (London: Hogarth Press, 1961), p.227.

4 Going rather against its logic, American artist Jeff Gagliardi makes shake-proof drawings of the Taj Mahal, Vitruvian Man and Queen of Hearts for example. In 2010 Etch A Sketch was revamped to mark its 50th anniversary, as a protective case for the iPad, with skeuomorphic white dials just for show.

Zephyros: the Book Untitled

Alan Loney & Miriam Morris, 2007
—acrylic ink, letterpress

The New Zealander Alan Loney, a consummate Olsenite poet, notebook keeper, letterpress printer and publisher in his own right, rejects the label 'artists' book' when it is applied to his work.[1] Loney is an adherent of the often time-consuming processes that go on in the physical settings of working life, his diverse back catalogue the result of an acute awareness of the manual relationship between type and text in a way that might seem old-fashioned, but ironically is also threatening to become ultra modern once again, the private press an example of burgeoning off-grid micro-culture, with dedicated followers and an Add to Basket button on its trade website.

> "Printing, like everything else, happens somewhere. In garages, living rooms, bedrooms, garden sheds, lofts, attics, art studios, universities, and nicely appointed special purpose printing shops, men and women have set up presses and trays of type and embarked on their hobby, recreation, avocation, vocation and their life's work in them."[2]

Zephyros: the Book Untitled has a double existence, published as chapter three of Loney's speculative collection of essays *The Books to Come* (2007)—its title a nod to Maurice Blanchot—and also as a fine press limited edition, with graphic verse or *technopeignia* as showcased in George Puttenham's *The Arte of English Poesie* (1589). *Zephyros* is embellished by a series of acrylic paintings courtesy of Miriam Morris. The Electio Editions description of *Zephyros*, an edition of thirty with twenty-six copies lettered A to Z for sale, is so seductive that it deservedly finds itself cited here, no longer a mere technical nicety, but part of the main body of this entry, the object's seductive range of typefaces, paper and paint worth a stand alone terminal slot in the text, as enticing as a box of handmade chocolates:

> "Paintings on Magnani mouldmade. Printings on Magnani mouldmade and Zerkall Nideggen mouldmade. Black, red, blue, and gold printing on Zerkall Nideggen mouldmade. Magnani sheets printed in black only. Types: Dante, Civilite, Libra, Franklin Gothic Greek, Open Kapitalen, Castellar. Bound in Cave handmade paper covered boards. In a red cloth-covered slipcase."[3]

1 A checklist of Loney's first fifty publications can be found in *The Private Library*, vol.10, no.4, winter 2007.

2 *The Printing of a Masterpiece* (Melbourne: Black Pepper Press, 2008), p.12.

3 See more at: www.vampandtramp.com/finepress/e/electio-editions.html

On Recent Tendencies in Bibliotecture: Memorials, Chutes and Shelving

Alain Resnais's documentary film essay *Toute la Mémoire du Monde*, 1956, sets out to narrate the passage of a single book through the holistic system of La Bibliothèque Nationale, Paris, as delineated against the grand architectonics of the library:

> "...a forbiddingly inhuman landscape in which man attempts to imprison 'knowledge' in an effort to counter the limits of his own memory. Only in the act of individual selection—a single patron choosing a specific text—is there hope that this undifferentiated mass of knowledge can be redeemed, as the reader makes discriminating use of the collective national memory for the fulfilment of a constructive individual purpose."[1]

The immediate context is sedimented: a bibliographic regime certain of its role as both archival container and dispenser of knowledge; its institutional hauteur a given. Resnais's flat commentary cites the restrictions placed upon the reader (and likewise the viewer), wherein the issued book is treated as a precious or antiquarian object, the basic unit with its catalogued data of Dewey decimal classification by discipline, shelfmark and description, namely size, year of publication, condition etc, to be closely protected day in, day out, against the possible abuse and innate criminality of the general public.[2]

However, the strict—even coercive—conventions that have been formulated and applied universally to storehouses of the manuscript, codex, newspaper micro-film and audiotape, in short the rules and regulations to which library readers are subject, have progressively been questioned, displaced and undermined since the late 1950s.[3] The inviolate authority of the printed word, and the unquestioned coherence of the book as sacred truth-bearing vessel, has come under multiple attack as a result of post-Nietzschean historical revisionism in the field of reading practice and the way text is both digested and marked, the irreversible seismic effect of the digital revolution, and a proliferation of so-called book art, sufficiently ubiquitous now to be considered a new variant or branch of sculpture.[4]

So within the unique space of contemporary visual art practice, the habitat of the public library has increasingly come to be seen as either an abstraction, interactive facility or neighbourhood hub, as in the collaborative 'social sculpture' of Michael Clegg and Martin Guttmann, whose work has often taken on the physical form and thus *dispositif* of the library and given it a cheeky twist in order to meddle with the site's behavioural codes. They like to speak of the "Trojan Horse" when characterising their work, such as *The Free Public Library*, 1990, *The Open Public Library*, 1993, and more recently the *Moebius Strip Library*, 2004, for instance, which was

> "...originally conceived for a presentation at the Waldzell Conference held in the Melk Abbey in 2004. In a generous elegant loop 2.8 metres tall and made of plywood, The Library has shelves that house writings by the Nobel Prize winners, academics, scientists and journalists who participated in the conference."[5]

With hindsight Buzz Spector's *The Library of Babel*, 1988, an arched structure made from 200 found books, must be considered a groundbreaking non-literary piece. From a similar era Anselm Kiefer's *Census*, 1991, an agglomerate of elephantine lead tomes housed in a shelving unit, possesses an apodictic force stemming not only from the mute density of lead as a material, but also the absence of any bookish characteristics such as jacket or titular information. *Census* puts the volume back into volumes, its cockled lead pages misleadingly delicate, and bafflingly illegible. On the other hand, Micha Ullman's *Library*, 1995, is an installation of empty lit shelves visible underground through a sunken glass plate at Bebelplatz, Berlin, recalling the Nazi book bonfires that took place on that spot in May, 1933. Ullman explains how

> "It begins with the void that exists in every pit and will not disappear. You could say that emptiness is a state, a situation formed by the sides of the pit: The deeper it is, the more sky there will be and the greater the void. In the library containing the missing books, that void is more palpable. We expect [the books] but they are not there."[6]

Massimo Bartolini's *Bookyard*, 2012, was a temporary outdoor library built and designed as part of Ghent's 'TRACK: A Contemporary City Conversation'.[7] Located in a small vineyard in St Peter's Abbey, its rows of wooden shelving, painted in a calming green tone, were aligned with adjacent rows of vines.

Books discarded from municipal libraries were for sale by voluntary donation. Kader Attia's more ambitious installation *The Continuum of Repair: The Light of Jacob's Ladder*, 2013,[8] featured North African learning boards or ketabs, and a plywood kiosk of erudite curiosities topped off with two large mirrors lit by a neon tube. Acting as reflectors, they shed a double image of the actual floor-to-ceiling shelving units jammed with scholarly reference books, as if the stacks went all the way to the stars.

> "...an in-depth engagement with the space as the reading room of the former Whitechapel library. It looks at the idea of books and objects as receptacles of history, continuously carrying memories with them. Attia links the trajectory of religious and scientific knowledge to the concept of repair, which he sees as an underlying principle of development and evolution."[9]

Yet despite the impressive scale and erudition of *Continuum*, this sort of accumulation can seem fatuous, as artist47365 commented online:

> "Attia is an interesting artist. But this is another show—a recent trend—to just collect up a load of stuff and let people work out the puzzle."[10]

Alicia Martin's amazing oeuvre is fully committed to the book as throwaway building block rather than literary or scientific text, resolving into almost unmanageable spills, doughnuts and exuberant defenestrating chutes. Fastened securely around a wire armature that allows their loose pages to flutter in the wind, what she calls "book streaming" is in effect a type of three-dimensional animation that recalls the stop-motion technique used by John Latham in experimental 16mm films like *Unclassified Material* and *Unedited Material from the Star*, both 1960—usually known as 'skoob' films—and so could be understood as a contemporary manifestation of Latham's concept of 'event structure'.

Rosie Leventon's *A Long Way from the Bathroom 2*, 1996, is artfully constructed from escapist romance novels, of the Mills & Boon,

Barbara Cartland variety, the suggestive concave space Leventon hollows out a reminder that

> "Beneath our too rationalised and civilised western world lie most of the things I am interested in—things such as archaeology, crop marks, iron age hill forts, long barrows. Also lost and buried watercourses, cisterns, and forgotten rivers. The piles of recycled paperbacks were piled up into stacks and the centre was hollowed out and carved into a saucer-like spherical negative shape."[11]

Her tower *Somewhere a Door Slams*, 2009, also uses recycled paperbacks to build an impressive shieling.

Australian-born duo Claire Healey & Sean Cordeiro's *Pulp Lack*, 2006, and *Word Lack*, 2006, both utilise books in a cavalier fashion, cutting them down to size specifically to fit IKEA's Lack shelving system. Made in Berlin, the books resemble Brechtian amputees, reminiscent of the dummy bookshelves used to hide secret passages or priest holes in old English manor houses. The concept of the library as a space to hide in, rather than a lending facility, figures too in Gayna Pelham's *Fully Booked*, 2007: 10,000 paperbacks randomly velcroed to walls, and used to line walk-through tunnels.[12]

Inevitably the constructivist re-purposing urge that drives many of these expanded uses of the book as brick, has itself already begun to look simplistic and a bit absurd, some of the larger structures imminently due to topple over: from Janet Cardiff & George Bures Miller's corbelled Wendy hut *The House of Books Has No Windows*, 2008, to Matej Krén's claustral *Passage*, 2005, from Columbian Miler Lagos's half finished book igloo *Home*, 2011, to Marta Minujin's hypertrophied, meretricious *Tower of Babel*, 2011, a seven storey helix using 30,000 books. Such an international rash of bling is in serious danger of provoking the "so what?" response.

In Xu Bing's highly controversial work *Book from the Sky*, 1988:

> "4,000 Chinese characters made as woodblock prints in the traditional canonical mode form an intensity of apparent signs that actually signify nonsense."[13]

Having spent four years labouring by hand over the pear wood blocks, Xu Bing successfully staged a mutation of Chinese history rather than its overturning, a xylographic act of truly formidable yet fragile bibliotecture. His unforgettable work is a further example of the library as contested site where identity and function is re-thought, re-engineered.

Christina Mitrentse's ongoing 'Add to My Library', very much a project for the digital age, conceives the library as a heterotopic manifold, a post-literary archive for imaginary users. Its dynamic representations range from A3 posters bearing BuzzFeed-like lists[14] of bibliographic data contributed by her fanbase, to gaily illuminated book mazes that double as durational performance venues, from screen prints of long-haired, saturnine bibliophiles, to boutique gallery obelisks made out of loose leaves removed from old school atlases, and from used paperbacks that have been shot with a Winchester 4.8 calibre rifle under licenced conditions, to coloured pencil and graphite drawings of global tourist destinations on the heritage trail: Stonehenge and Tate Modern knocked up from popular hardbacks, a temenos and ziggurat of artfully selected ISBNs. As Peter Suchin has remarked of her work

> "…the utopia of the library has become the dystopia of cultural ruin, decline, desecration".[15]

And indeed such entropic devastation is the focus of James D. Griffion's astonishing photographs of the Detroit Public Schools Book Depository, where matted layers of abandoned books are captured at the point of utter disintegration into powdery spores, a rotting information dump and North American dustbowl for our times.

> "Mushrooms thrive in the damp ashes of workbooks. Box Elders and *Ailanthus altissima*—the 'ghetto palm'—grow through holes in the ceiling from a soil made by thousands of books that have burned, and in the pulp of rotted English Textbooks. Everything of any real value has been looted."[16]

The counter-movement against such wanton neglect, and a means to re-activate elderly stock occupying valuable shelf space, are projects such as 'Regenerator I & II',[17] 'The Library of Lost Books'[18] and Irmari Nacht's 'Saved', 2015. This outbreak of lateral thinking which lies behind the act of making discards available for re-tread creates new circulating libraries based on exhumation and metamorphosis rather than the typical withdrawn sale at municipal library level, where frontispieces are ripped out by staff in order to destroy unwanted stock's sell-on value to dealers.

Such adornments of a library serve as prosthetic extensions to its main body, as too does performance art, which has tentatively begun to taken up residence in the hard-to-police cubby holes and vennels of bibliographic space. Marie Ann O'Neill's *Athenæum Exploration* and Keli Emery's *Library Orienteering* were part of the group exhibition 'The Artist in the Library', 2011.[19] O'Neill's dance piece evolved from her close observation of the gestures peculiar to library users, leading to choreographic interventions in stair wells and on landings. Emery deposited a series of quotations inside scattered books, her work implemented by browsers making chance discoveries.

Jennie Savage's audio piece *A Walk from A-Z*, 2010, was designed for Lancaster Library, a place with links to Chartist agitation. Savage sees the library as a threatened site of self-improvement and resistance. She is openly critical of

> "…neo-liberal ideology that combines a curious mix of corporate branding and flimsy ideals of openness and community but fails to deal with the fundamental issues of inequality or exclusion within a society at large. Using art or, in this case libraries, as a sticking plaster to cover its failure to actually deal with issues of poverty, breakdown of family and poor levels of education."[20]

Re-design of library fixtures, fittings and *meubles* has also become a rich source of invention. Commissioned by onestar press for their OSB collection (the publisher's website loudly proclaims "Shelter your books in exciting new homes…"),[21] artists such as Lawrence Weiner, Elvira Bonduelle and Annika Ström have applied themselves to the practical task of shelf design. Weiner's plywood reference bookcase bears the slogan EMPOWERMENT CANNOT BE TRANSLATED AS ENTITLEMENT, while Bonduelle's hand-painted *Cale/Wedge*, 2003–2013, is a charming design solution:

> "Les Cales, sorte d'objet en mousse de couleur douteuse, permettent à l'artiste d'arrondir les angles, de se lover confortablement, de revisiter le mobilier urbain ou de créer des sculptures éphémères entre espace intime et espace public."[22]

Ström's elegant *Bookshelf Monuments Made in France*, 2010, are loosely based on that most underrated, versatile piece of furniture, the hallstand. Andres Ayerbe Posada and Camille Leproust aka NOOT however show no mercy, or sentiment, for Primary School furniture in their piece *Desk & Bench*, 2014, that was commissioned for the project 'Unbinding the Book',[23] as its user witnesses the slow darkening into illegibility of a book of poems printed on thermal paper.

Mel Jackson's occult-themed accordion book *The Brazen Oracle* (1997) and Allen Ruppersberg's web-based *The New Five Foot Shelf of Books*, 2003,[24] a record of his former studio at 611 Broadway, compress the physical library in a *multum in parvo* gesture, while Amanda Andersen's *Page Count* (2011), an exercise in metonymic indexing, uses the page as a key, and referential prompt:

> "A documentation of all the books Andersen owns, arranged in order of page counts and represented by respective page numbers."[25]

Coming full circle, Ant Hampton and Tim Etchell's *The Quiet Volume*, 2011, operates below the radar, a whispered automatic performance for two readers, who in effect become protagonists, offering a technologically intimate way of navigating book-lined rooms, one worlds away in its seductive proprioception from the chilly universe depicted by Resnais, and effectively date stamping a historical shift and transvaluation stretching from aloof academic reader to researcher/user/player. So the dizziness adduced by Patrick Hughes' "reverspective" painting of monolithic library stacks *Paradoxymoron*, 1996, permanently on display in the lower ground floor of the British Library, London, is the result not only of perceptual warping, but also a subliminal fear that the physical library will be rendered defunct, its contents destroyed,[26] time irrevocably ruptured,[27] a scenario investigated in Rachel Tweddell's project 'Books Thrown with Great Force', 2013, action giclée prints of sundry paperbacks being violently hurled into sheer space.[28]

Ruth Beale's melancholy audio work *Now from Now*, 2011, addresses a future break down of order too:

> "A narrative monologue describing a journey through a fictional out-of-time London where all libraries are closed, but where the methodical exploration of the boarded-up relics is disrupted by acid trip-outs and sublime moments. It is exhibited as a sound

> piece with a bookshelf of over sixty utopian novels on loan from London Libraries. A live version is performed with a liquid light show projection."[29]

Katrina Palmer is less concerned with an apocalyptic future, but chooses to play with the idea of an absence of books, and it is this spectral possibility that focuses and haunts her text *A Perverse Transposition* (2012):

> "The bookcase is empty, laying on its side, horizontally along the floor. Had there been any books they would be stacked directly on top of each other as the shelves are now vertical slots."[30]

From authoritarian, quaint, disciplinary to immersive and digital, the library as recognisable pedagogic institution is nevertheless still the conservative double to many of the idiosyncratic structures cited in this appendix.

But of course there are still those spokesmen who long for the fabled atmosphere of an *ancien régime* municipal library:

> "Modern (though extremely useful) technology, and design is rather cool and detached compared to the old style library of card index drawers, wooden shelves with carved finials, loan stamps, low-level lighting, hushed voices, etc."[31]

Such nostalgia haunts our torn epoch.

Notes

1 www.aschenker.blogspot.co.uk/2008/03/toute-la-m-du-monde.html

2 'The Private Lives of Print: The Use and Abuse of Books 1450–1550', at the Milstein Exhibition Centre, Cambridge, 24 October–11 April 2014/15, demonstrated how early modern reading practices such as doodling and marginal annotation were vital to scholarly interaction with texts.

3 Consider for instance the Lawrence Alloway curated exhibition 'Theo Crosby: Sculpture, Peter Blake: Objects, John Latham: Libraries', ICA, London W1, 7–30 January 1960.

4 Although the term 'quasi-sculpture' is occasionally used when referring to modified, disbound book structures or public art made from books, this is by no means pejorative, simply indicating the materials are non-classical in origin.

5 www.viennareview.net/on-the-town/on-display/clegg-guttmann-unraveling-codes-of-status

6 www.en.wikipedia.or/wiki/micha_Ullman

7 12 May–16 September 2012.

8 Whitechapel Gallery, London E1, 26 November 2013–23 November 2014.

9 www.whitechapelgallery.org/downloads/Exhibs_KaderAttia_InterpPanelsx2_22NovPRINT_filmcred1.pdf

10 www.theguardian.com/artanddesign/2013/dec/15/kader-attia-jacobs-ladder-review-whitechapel

11 www.rosieleventon.com/recycled-sculpture/art-installation-A-LONG-WAY.html

12 Novas Contemporary Urban Centre, London SE1, September–October 2007.

13 Stephen Lee, 'Xu Bing: Landscape Landscript', *Art Monthly*, no.365, April 2013.

14 "The paradox of Mitrentse's project is that it is both a sign of dissipation, of the loss of knowledge and the means for its transmission, and a conscious recouping or preservation of the culture of the book." Peter Suchin, exhibition notes, 'Book upon Book upon Book: Christina Mitrentse', 'Add to My Library' vol.II, Art Work Space, The Hempel Hotel, London W2, 29 August–25 September 2011.

15 Ibid.

16 www.jamesgriffioen.com

17 Launched in February 2010 at Bower Ashton Library, Bristol. www.bookarts.uwe.ac.uk/news-archive/regen10/index.htm

18 The Pavilion, Library of Birmingham, 6–24 November 2013. www.thelibraryoflostbooks.blogspot.co.uk

19 Mayfest, Docklands Campus, University of East London, 2011.

20 www.jenniesavage.co.uk/walk%20az/walka_z.htm

21 www.onestarpress.com/NEWSLETTER/bookshelves-from-osp

22 "Les Cales—subtly coloured foam shapes—let the artist cut corners, curl up in comfort, serving as urban decor or temporary sculpture fashioned between private and public space." www.elvirebonduelle.com/en/by-claire-staebler/

23 unbindingthebook.com

24 Originally published in 2001, it was labelled NOT FOR SALE due to the impossibility of paying royalties for every quotation it contained. Ruppersberg's book references *Dr Eliot's Five Foot Shelf of Books* (1910), a Harvard Classic collection of fifty books indispensable to gentlemen.

25 www.amanda-andersen.com

26 In Daniel Knorr's work *State of Mind*, 2007, a pile of fake rocks made from pulped Stasi files, geo-political rupturing is integral, and to be embraced.

27 'Oh, Zero, One', Cell Project Space, London E2, 18 November–18 December 2011. This two-person exhibition also included a video by Una Knox about an epileptic 'gatekeeper' meandering through the forbidding store rooms of an ultramodern library.

28 Westminster Reference Library, London WC2, 15-27 March 2013.

29 http://ruthbeale.net/work/now-from-now

30 Text commissioned for the *London Book Map*, no.2 (2012).

31 gistofthegrist.wordpress.com/2014/08/12/heaven

APPENDIX II

Select Bibliography

Adamson, Glenn, *Thinking Through Craft* (Oxford/London: Berg 3PL & V&A Publishing, 2007)

Alberro, Alexander, *Conceptual Art and the Politics of Publicity* (Cambridge, MA/London: The MIT Press, 2003)

Alexander, Jonathan J. G., *Medieval Illuminators and Their Methods of Work* (New Haven, CT/London: Yale University Press, 1992)

Allen, Gwen, *Artists' Magazines: An Alternative Space for Art* (Cambridge, MA/London: MIT Press, 2011)

Alliez, Éric and Peter Osborne, *Spheres of Action: Art and Politics* (London: Tate Publishing, 2013)

Amerika, Mark, *remixthebook* (Minneapolis, MN: University of Minnesota Press, 2011)

Andrews, Malcolm, *The Search for the Picturesque: Landscape Aesthetics and Tourism in Britain, 1760–1800* (Aldershot: Scolar Press, 1989)

Antaya, Christine, *Book Art: Iconic Sculptures and Installations Made from Books* (Berlin: Gestalten, 2011)

Aranda, Juliet, Brian Kuan Wood and Anton Vidokle (eds.), *Are You Working Too Much? Post-Fordism, Precarity and the Labor of Art* (Berlin: Sternberg Press, 2011)

Arkhiov, Vladimir, *Home Made: Contemporary Russian Folk Artifacts* (London: Fuel, 2006)

Arnar, Anna Sigrídur, *The Book as Instrument: Stephane Mallarmé, the Artist's Book, and the Transformation of Print Culture* (Chicago, IL/London: University of Chicago Press, 2011)

Aronow, Edward and Marvin Reznikoff, *Rorschach Content Interpretation* (New York, NY: Grune & Stratton, 1976)

Ascott, Roy, *Telematic Embrace: Visionary Theories of Art, Technology, and Consciousness* (Berkeley, CA: University of California Press, 2003)

Ash, Lee, *Book Arts Collections: A Representative Selection* (New York, NY: Haworth Press, 1989)

Ash, Russell and Brian Lake, *Bizarre Books* (London: Pavilion, 1998)

Atwood, Martin and Clive Phillpot (eds.), *Artists' Books* (London: Arts Council of Great Britain, 1976)

Augé, Marc, *Non-Places: An Introduction to Supermodernity* (London/New York, NY: Verso, 2009)

Badger, Gerry and Martin Parr, *The Photobook: A History, Vols I–III* (London: Phaidon, 2004, 2006, 2014)

Bahn, Paul G. and Jean Vertut, *Journey Through the Ice Age* (London: Weidenfeld & Nicholson, 1997)

Bailey, Stewart, and David Reinfurt, *The Serving Library* (Berlin: Sternberg Press, 2011)

Banham, Reyner, *Theory and Design in the First Machine Age* (London: Architectural Press, 1960)

Bann, Stephen (ed.), *Interlacing Words and Things: Bridging the Nature-Culture Opposition in Gardens and Landscape* (Washington, DC: Dumbarton Oaks Research Library and Collection, 2012)

Barbier, Carl Paul, *William Gilpin: His Drawings, Teaching and Theory of the Picturesque* (Oxford: Clarendon Press, 1963)

Barker, Nicolas, *Form and Meaning in the History of the Book* (London: British Library, 2003)

——, *The Butterfly Books: An Enquiry into the Nature of Certain Twentieth Century Pamphlets* (London: Bertram Rota, 1987)

Barker, Ronald E., *Photocopying Practices in the United Kingdom* (London: Faber & Faber, 1970)

Barton, Carol June and Henry Barrow, *Books and Bookends: Sculptural Approaches, 1989–1991* (Bethesda, MD: Popular Kinetics Press, 1990)

Bayard, Pierre, *How to Talk About Books You Haven't Read* (London: Granta, 2007)

Baynton-Williams, Roger, *The Art of the Printmaker* (London: A. & C. Black, 2009)

Bazarnik, Katarzyna and Izabella Curyllo-Klag (eds.), *Incarnations of Material Textuality from Modernism to Literature* (Newcastle-upon-Tyne: Cambridge Scholars, 2014)

Béchard-Léauté, Anne and Valentin Oncin, *Le Livre D'Artiste depuis 1980 en France et au Royaume-Unis* (St Etienne: Presses Universitaires, 2014)

Beck, John and Matthew Cornford, *The Art School and the Culture Shed* (Kingston upon Thames: The Centre for Useless Splendour, 2013)

Bergler, Edmund, *The Talent for Stupidity: The Psychology of the Bungler, the Incompetent, and the Ineffectual* (Madison, CT: International Universities Press, 1998)

Bervin, Jen, Marta Werner and Susan Howe (eds.), *The Gorgeous Nothings: Emily Dickenson's Envelope Poems* (New York, NY: New Directions & Christine Burgin, 2013)

Bick, Andrew, *Books as Art* (Gloucestershire: University of Gloucestershire, 1998)

Bing, Xu, *Passages in the Making of a Book* (London: Bernard Quaritch, 2009)

Blamey, David, (ed.), *Work and Turn: Artists' Bookworks from the United Kingdom* (London: Open Editions, 1992)

Bland, David, *A History of Book Illustration* (London: Faber, 1958)

Bleus, Guy, *Art is Books: Artists' Books* (Hasselt: PCOB, 1990)

Bodman, Sarah, *Creating Artists' Books* (London: A. & C. Black, 2005)

Bolt, Roelf, *The Encyclopaedia of Liars and Deceivers* (London: Reaktion Books, 2014)

Boltanski, Christian and Catherine Grenier (ed.), *The Possible Life of Christian Boltanski* (Boston, MA: MFA Publications, 2009)

Bolter, Jay David, *Writing Space: The Computer, Hypertext, and the History of Writing* (Hillsdale, NJ: Lawrence Erlbaum Associates, 1991)

——, and Richard Grusin, *Remediation: Understanding New Media* (Cambridge, MA/ London: MIT Press, 2000)

Bosse, Claudia (ed.), *Cheap Methods Edition: Struggling Bodies in Capitalist Societies (Democracies)* (Vienna/Berlin: theatrecombinat & Motto Books, 2012)

Bovier, Lionel and Christophe Cherix, *Ecart* (1969–1980) (Zurich: JRP Ringier, 2013)

Bowkett, Steve, *Archidoodle: An Architect's Activity Book* (London: Laurence King, 2013)

Bowman, Alan T. and J. D. Thomas, *Vindolanda: the Latin Writing Tablets* (London: Britannia Monograph Series, IV, 1983)

Braidotti, Rosi, *The Posthuman* (Cambridge: Polity Press, 2013)

Brassier, Ray, *Nihil Unbound: Enlightenment and Extinction* (Basingstoke: Palgrave Macmillan, 2010)

Brayman-Hackel, Heidi, *Reading Material in Early Modern England: Print, Gender and Literacy* (Cambridge: Cambridge University Press, 2005)

Breakwell, Ian and Paul Hammond, *Brought to Book* (London: Penguin, 1994)

Brennan, Tim, *The Curationist Manifesto* (York: Information as Material, 2003)

Briers, David, *Groove: Artists and Vinyl* (Huddersfield: Huddersfield Art Gallery, 2002)

Bright, Betty, *No Longer Innocent: Book Art in America* (New York, NY: Granary Books, 2002)

Britton, Tessy, *Hand Made: Portraits of Emergent New Community Culture* (Self-Published, 2010)

Brouws, Jeff, Wendy Burton and Hermann Zschiegner, *Various Small Books: Referencing Various Small Books by Ed Ruscha* (Cambridge, MA/London: MIT Press, 2013)

Bruno, Giordano and Dick Higgins (ed.), Charles Doria (trans.), *On the Composition of Images, Signs & Ideas* (New York, NY: Willis, Locker & Owens, 1991)

Brus, Gunter, (ed.), *Die Schastrommel* 1–12 (Berlin: Self-Published/Verlag Interfunktionen/Verlag Hansjorg Mayer, 1969–1974)

Buchloh, Benjamin (ed.), *Interfunktionen* 11 (Cologne: Verlag Heubach, 1974)

Burgin, Victor, *The Remembered Film* (London: Reaktion Books, 2004)

Bury, Stephen, *Artist's Multiples 1935–2000* (London: Ashgate Publishing Company, 2002)

Bryant, Julius, Elizabeth James and Rowan Watson, *Word & Image: Art, Books and Design from the National Art Library* (London: V&A Publishing, 2014)

Cadôr, Amir Brito, *A Night Visit to the Library* (Belo Horizonte: Andante Editions, 2013)

Cage, John, *Silence: Lectures & Writings* (Middletown, CT: Wesleyan University Press, 1961)

Calle, Bob, *Christian Boltanski: Artist's Books 1969–2007* (Paris: Editions 591, 2008)

Campbell, Eddie, *The Fate of the Artist* (New York, NY: First Second, 2006)

Campbell, Natalie (ed.), *Artists' Books as (Sub) Culture* (New York, NY: The Center for Book Arts, 2009)

Cardinal, Roger and J Elsner (eds.), *The Cultures of Collecting* (London: Reaktion Books, 1994)

Carr, Nicholas, *The Shallows: How the Internet is Changing the Way We Read, Think and Remember* (London: Atlantic Books, 2010)

Carrier, David and Joachim Pissarro, *Wild Art* (London: Phaidon, 2013)

Carrión, Ulises (ed.), *Van Kunstenaarsboeken tot Postkunst/From Bookworks to Mailworks* (Amsterdam: Alkmaar Municipal Museum, 1978)

——, *Second Thoughts* (Amsterdam: Void Distributors, 1980)

Carter, S. Gilmour (ed.), *Paper: Its Making, Merchanting and Usage* (London: NAPM and Longmans, Green & Co., 1956)

Castle, Egerton, *English Book-Plates, Ancient and Modern* (London/New York, NY: George Bell & Sons, 1893)

Cave, Roderick, *The Private Press* (New York: Watson-Guptill Publications, 1971)

Celant, Germano and Lynda Morris (eds.), *Book as Artwork 1960/1972* (London: Nigel Greenwood, 1972)

Chan, Paul, *Wht is a Book?* (New York, NY: Badlands Unlimited, 2011)*

Chapon, François, *Le Peintre et le Livre: L'Age d'Or du Livre Illustré en France 1870–1970* (Paris: Flammarion, 1987)

Chiplis, Martha and Cathie Ruggie Saunders, *For the Love of Letterpress: A Printing Handbook for Instructors and Students* (London: Bloomsbury, 2013)

Clanchy, Michael T., *From Memory to Written Record: England 1066–1307* (London: Edward Arnold, 1979)

Clay, Steven (ed.), *When Will the Book Be Done?: Granary's Books* (New York, NY: Granary Books, 2001)

Cockerell, Douglas, *Bookbinding and the Care of Books: A Handbook for Amateurs, Bookbinders and Librarians* (New York, NY: D. Appleton & Co., 1901)

Coe, Jonathan, *Like a Fiery Elephant: The Story of B. S. Johnson* (London: Picador, 2005)

Cohen, Stanley and Laurie Taylor, *Escape Attempts: The Theory and Practice of Resistance to Everyday Life* (London: Allen Lane, 1976)

Colsell, Ilsa, *Malicious Damage: the Defaced Library Books of Kenneth Halliwell & Joe Orton* (London: Donlon Books, 2013)

Compton, Susan P., *The World Backwards: Russian Futurist Books 1912–16* (London: The British Library, 1978)

Connolly, William E., *The Fragility of Things: Self-Organizing Processes, Neoliberal Fantasies, and Democratic Activism* (Durham, NC: Duke University Press, 2013)

Connor, Steven, *Paraphernalia* (London: Profile Books, 2012)

Cook, Jill, *Ice Age Art: the Arrival of the Modern Mind* (London: The British Museum Press, 2013)

Copley, Anthony, *Wits, Fittes and Fancies* (London: Edward Allde, 1614)

Courtney, Cathy, *Speaking of Book Art: Interviews with British and American Book Artists* (Los Altos Hills, CA: Anderson-Lovelace, 1999)

——, *The Looking Book: A Pocket History of Circle Press 1967–96* (London: Circle Press, 1996)

——, *Private Views & Other Containers: Artists' Books Reviewed by Cathy Courtney for Art Monthly* (London: Estamp, 1992)

Coxhead, David and Susan Hiller, *Dreams: Visions of the Night* (New York, NY: Thames & Hudson, 1989)

Crary, Jonathan, *24/7: Late Capitalism and the Ends of Sleep* (London/New York, NY: Verso, 2013)

Critton, Benjamin (ed.), *Five Years* (Brighton: Colophon Foundry, 2014)

Cutts, Simon, *Some Forms of Availability: Critical Passages on the Book and Publication* (New York/Derby: Granary Books/RGAP, 2007)

—— (ed.), *Certain Trees: The Constructed Book, Poem and Object 1964–2006* (Saint-Yrieix-la-Perche: CDLA, 2006)

—— (ed.), *The Coracle: Coracle Press Gallery 1975–1987* (London: Coracle Press, 1989)

Darling, Jesse, *Back Catalogue* (Self-Published, 2012)

Daston, Lorraine and Katharine Park *Wonders and the Order of Nature 1150–1750* (Brooklyn, NY: Zone Books, 2001)

Davidts, Wouter and Kim Paice (eds.), *The Fall of the Studio* (Amsterdam: Valiz, 2009)

Dean, Deborah, *Lace: Here: Now* (London: Black Dog, 2013)

Debord, Guy and Alice Becker-Ho, *A Game of War* (London: Atlas Press, 2007)

De Forest, Tim, *Storytelling in the Pulps, Comics and Radio: How Technology Changed Popular Fiction in America* (Jefferson, NC: McFarlane & Co., 2004)

Deleuze, Gilles, Barbara Habberjam and Hugh Tomlinson (trans.), *Bergsonism* (Brooklyn, NY: Zone Books, 1988)

Deller, Jeremy and Alan Kane, *Folk Archive: Contemporary Popular Art from the UK* (Opus Projects) (London: Book Works, 2005)

Desjardin, Arnaud, *The Book on Books on Artists' Books* (London: The Everyday Press, 2011)

Detterer, Gabriele and Maurizio Nannucci (eds.), *Artist-Run Spaces: Non-Profit Collective Organizations in the 1960s and 1970s* (Zurich: JRP Ringier, 2012)

Dressen, Anne (ed.), *Elaine Sturtevant: The Razzle Dazzle of Thinking* (Zurich: JRP Ringier, 2010)

Drucker, Johanna, *The Century of Artists' Books* (New York, NY: Granary Books, 1995)

——, *Figuring the Word: Essays on Books, Writing and Visual Poetics* (New York, NY: Granary Books, 1988)

——, *The Visible Word: Experimental Typography and Modern Art, 1909–1923* (Chicago, IL: Chicago University Press, 1994)

——, Anne Mœglin-Delcroix and Tania Orum, *Danish Artists' Books* (Cologne: Walther Konig, 2014)

Dûval, William with Valerie Monahan, *Collecting Postcards in Colour 1894–1914* (Poole: Blandford Press, 1978)

Dworkin, Craig, *No Media* (Cambridge, MA/ London: The MIT Press, 2013)

——, *The Perverse Library* (York: Information as Material, 2010)

Earle, David M., *Re-Covering Modernism: Pulps, Paperbacks and the Prejudice of Form* (Farnham: Ashgate, 2009)

Easton, Phoebe Jane, *Marbling: A History and a Bibliography* (Los Angeles, CA: Dawson's Book Shop, 1983)

Eco, Umberto and Jean-Claude Carrière, *This is Not the End of the Book* (London: Harvill Secker, 2011)

Eisenstein, Elisabeth, *The Printing Press as an Agent of Change* (Cambridge: Cambridge University Press, 1979)

Ellery, Jonathan, *136 Points of Reference* (London: Ellery/Browns/Westerham Press, 2005)

Elser, Oliver and Peter Cachola Schmal (eds.), *The Architectural Model: Tool, Fetish, Small Utopia* (Zurich: Park Books, 2012)

Entzenberg, Claes, *Art from Death Originated* (Amsterdam: Idea Books, 2013)

Erasmus, Desiderius, *De Copia* (Paris: Josse Bade, 1512)

Evans, Robert J. W., *Rudolf II and His World: A Study in Intellectual History, 1576–1612* (Oxford: Clarendon Press, 1973)

Eyres, Patrick, *The New Arcadians: An Introduction to the Tarasque, Coracle and New Arcadian Presses* (Washington, DC: Dumbarton Oaks, Research Library Catalogue, 2009)

Fairman, Elisabeth R. (ed.), *Of Green Leaf, Bird, and Flower: Artists' Books and the Natural World* (New Haven, CT/London: Yale University Press, 2014)

Farrelly, Liz, *Zines* (London: Booth-Clibborn, 2001)

Feather, John and Graham Matthews (eds.), *Disaster Management for Libraries and Archives* (Farnham: Ashgate, 2003)

Filliou, Robert, *Teaching and Learning as Performing Arts* (London: Occasional Papers, 2014)

Finlay, Alec (ed.), *The Libraries of Thought and Imagination* (Edinburgh: Polygon, 2002)

Fishburn, Matthew, *Burning Books* (Basingstoke: Palgrave Macmillan, 2008)

Flay, Jennifer (ed.), *Christian Boltanski: Catalogue: Books, Printed Matter, Ephemera 1966–1991* (Cologne: Walter König, 1992)

Fleming, Juliet, *Graffiti & the Writing Arts in Early Modern England* (London: Reaktion Books, 2001)

Flusser, Vilém, Nancy Ann Roth (trans.), *Does Writing Have a Future?* (Minneapolis, MN: University of Minnesota Press, 2011)

Frank, Joseph, *The Beginnings of the English Newspaper 1620–1660* (Cambridge, MA: Harvard University Press, 1961)

Freeman, Rosemary, *English Emblem Books* (London: Chatto & Windus, 1948)

Friedberg, Anne, *The Virtual Window: From Alberti to Microsoft* (Cambridge, MA: MIT Press, 2006)

Frigge, Karli and Els Rademacher, *Sample Book of the Fancy Papers Factory Aschaffenburg* (Buren: Frits Knuf, 1993)

Fusco, Maria and Ian Hunt (eds.), *Put About: A Critical Anthology of Independent Publishing* (London: Book Works, 2004)

Garrett, Stewart, *Bookwork: Medium to Object to Concept to Art* (Chicago, IL/ London: The University of Chicago Press, 2011)

Gass, William H., *A Temple of Texts* (New York, NY: Alfred A. Knopf, 2006)

Gauntlett, David, *Making is Connecting: The Social Meaning of Creativity, from DIY and Knitting to YouTube and Web 2.0* (Cambridge: Polity Press, 2011)

Genette, Gérard, Jane E. Lewin (trans.), *Paratexts: Thresholds of Interpretation* (Cambridge: Cambridge University Press, 1997)

Gilbert, Annette, Uljana Wolf (trans.), *Re-Print: Appropriation (&) Literature* (Wiesbaden: Luxbooks, 2014)

Gill, Eric, *An Essay on Typography* (Boston, MA: David R Godine, 1993)

Gitelman, Lisa, *Paper Knowledge: Towards a Media History of Documents (Sign, Storage, Transmission)* (Durham, NC: Duke University Press, 2014)

——, and Pingree, Geoffrey B., *New Media 1740–1915* (Cambridge, MA/London: MIT Press, 2004)

Görtschacher, Wolfgang, *The Underground Alternative Press in Britain: A Bibliographical Guide with Historical Notes* (Hassocks: Harvester Press, 1993)

Gray, Alasdair, *The Book of Prefaces* (London: Bloomsbury Publishing, 2000)

Green, Jonathon, *Days in the Life: Voices from the English Underground 1961–1971* (London/Portsmouth, NH: William Heinemann, 1988)

Greenspan, Alan, *The Age of Turbulence* (London: Penguin Press, 2007)

Grunenberg, Cristoph (ed.), *Summer of Love: Art of the Psychedelic Era* (London: Tate Publishing, 2005)

Guest, Tim and Germano Celant, *Books by Artists* (Toronto: Art Metropole 1981)

Guthrie, Derek (ed.), *The New Art Examiner*, vol.26, no.3 November 1998 (Chicago, IL: Chicago New Art Association)

Haebler, Konrad, L. E. Osborne (trans.), *The Study of Incunabula* (New York, NY: Grolier Club, 1933)

Haining, Peter, *The Classic Era of American Pulp Magazines* (Chicago, IL: Chicago Review Press, 2001)

——, *Movable Books: An Illustrated History* (London: New English Library, 1979)

Hainley, Bruce, *Under the Sign of (sic): Sturtevant's Volte-Face* (Los Angeles, CA: Semiotext(e), 2013)

Halasz, Alexandra, *The Marketplace of Print: Pamphlets and the Public Sphere in Early Modern England* (Cambridge: Cambridge University Press, 1997)

Hall, Gary, *Digitize this Book: The Politics of New Media, or Why We Need Open Access Now* (Minneapolis, MN/London: University of Minnesota Press, 2008)

Halliday, Nigel Vaux, *More Than a Bookshop: Zwemmer's and Art in the 20th Century* (London: Philip Wilson Publishers, 2003)

Hamady, Walter, *Papermaking by Hand: A Book of Suspicions* (Dane County, WI: The Perishable Press)

Harmon, Katharine, *The Map as Art: Contemporary Artists Explore Cartography* (New York, NY: Princeton Architectural Press, 2010)

——, *You Are Here: Personal Geographies and Other Maps of the Imagination* (New York, NY: Princeton Architectural Press, 2004)

Harris, Michael and Robin Myers (eds.), *A Millenium of the Book: Production, Design and Illustration in Print, 900–1900* (Winchester/ New Castle, DE: St Paul's Bibliographies and Oak Knoll Press, 1994)

Haskell, Francis, *The Painful Birth of the Art Book* (London: Thames & Hudson, 1987)

Hayles, Katherine N., *Writing Machines* (Cambridge, MA/London: MIT Press, 2002)

Helfand, Jessica, Scrapbooks: *An American History* (New Haven, CT/London: Yale University Press, 2008)

——, *Reinventing the Wheel: Volvelles, Equatoria, Planispheres, Fact-Finders, Gestational Charts…* (New York, NY: Princeton Architectural Press, 2002)

Hellyer, Peter, (ed.), *A Catalogue of Russian Avant-Garde Books 1912–1934 and 1969–2003* (London: The British Library, 2006)

Henderson, Linda Dalrymple, *The Fourth Dimension and Non-Euclidean Geometry in Modern Art* (Princeton, NJ: Princeton University Press, 1983)

Heninger, S. K. Jr, *The Cosmographical Glass: Renaissance Diagrams of the Universe* (San Marino, CA: Huntington Library Press, 2005)

Herring, Ann, *The World of Chiyogami* (Tokyo/ New York, NY: Kodansha Amer Inc, 1987)

Higgins, Charlotte, *Under Another Sky: Journeys in Roman Britain* (London: Jonathan Cape, 2012)

Higgins, Dick and Charles Alexander (ed.), *Talking the Boundless Book: Art, Language, & the Book Arts* (Minneapolis, MN: Minnesota Center for Book Arts, 1995)

Higgins, Hannah and Douglas Kahn (eds.), *Mainframe Experimentalism: Early Computing and the Foundation of the Digital Arts* (Berkeley, CA: University of California Press, 2012)

Hill, Craig and Niko Vassilakis (eds.), *The Last Vispo Anthology 1998–2008* (Seattle, WA: Fantagraphics, 2012)

Hobsbawm, Eric, *Fractured Times: Culture and Society in the 20th Century* (New York, NY: Little, Brown, 2013)

Hoffmann, Jens, *Ten Fundamental Questions of Curating* (London: Fiorucci Trust, 2013)

Home, Stewart (ed.), *What is Situationism? A Reader* (Edinburgh: AK Press, 1996)

Houston, Keith, *Shady Characters: Ampersands, Interrobangs and Other Typographic Curiosities* (London: Particular Books, 2013)

Hubert, Renée Riese (guest ed.), *Visible Language*, vol.25, 2/3 (Providence, RI: Rhode Island School of Design, 1991)

—— (guest ed.) *SubStance*, vol.26, no.1 Issue 82, Special Issue: Metamorphosis of the Book (Madison, WI: University of Wisconsin Press, 1997)

——, *Surrealism and the Book* (Oakland, CA: The University of California Press, 1988)

——, and Judd D. Hubert, *The Cutting Edge of Reading: Artists' Books* (New York, NY: Granary Books, 1999)

Hudek, Antony and Athanasios Velios, *The Portable John Latham* (London: Occasional Papers, 2010)

Hulme, Edward F., *Suggestions in Floral Design* (London/Paris/New York, NY: Cassell, Petter & Galpin, 1878)

Hunt, Ian and Jane Rolo (eds.), *Book Works: A Partial History and Sourcebook* (London: Book Works, 1996)

Hunt, W. M., *The Unseen Eye: Photographs from the Unconscious* (London: Thames & Hudson, 2011)

Iliazd, *Poésie Des Mots Inconnus* (Paris: Le Degré 41, 1949)

Imelli, Al, *The Book of Alphabets and Layouts: The Art of Metal Etching for Sign Purposes* (Cincinnati, OH: The Signs of the Times Publishing Company, 1922)

Ingold, Tim, *Making: Anthropology, Archaeology, Art and Architecture* (Abingdon: Routledge, 2013)

——, *Lines: A Brief History* (London: Routledge, 2007)

Isselbacher, Audrey (ed.), *Iliazd and the Illustrated Book* (New York, NY: MOMA, 1987)

Jacobs, Frank, *Strange Maps: An Atlas of Cartographic Curiosities* (New York, NY: Viking Press, 2009)

Janacek, Gerald, *Zaum: The Transrational Language of Russian Futurism* (San Diego, CA: San Diego State University Press, 1996)

Janik, Allan and Stephen Toulmin, *Wittgenstein's Vienna* (New York, NY: Simon & Schuster, 1973)

Jencks, Charles and Nathan Silver, *Adhocism: The Case for Improvisation* (Cambridge, MA/ London: MIT Press, 2013)

Jennings, Michael W. and Detlef Mertins (eds.), *G: An Avant-Garde Journal of Art, Architecture, Design, & Film, 1923–1926* (Los Angeles, CA: Getty Research Institute, 2010)

Jensen, Kristian (ed.), *Incunabula and Their Readers: Printing, Selling, and Using Books in the Fifteenth Century* (London: British Library, 2003)

Johns, Adrian, *The Nature of the Book: Print and Knowledge in the Making* (Chicago, IL/ London: University of Chicago, 1998)

Johnston, Alastair M, *Hanging Quotes: Talking Book Arts, Typography and Poetry* (Victoria, TX: Cuneiform Press, 2011)

Jones, Gerard, *Men of Tomorrow: Geeks, Gangsters and the Birth of the Comic* (New York, NY: Basic Books, 2005)

Jones, Owen, *The Grammar of Ornament* (London: Day & Son, 1856)

Joselit, David, *After Art* (Princeton, NJ: Princeton University Press, 2012)

Kaneko, Ryuichi and Ivan Vartanian, *Japanese Photobooks of the 1960s and 70s* (New York, NY: Aperture, 2009)

Kaprow, Allan and Jeff Kelley (ed.), *Essays on the Blurring of Art and Life* (Oakland, CA: University of California Press, 2003)

Keen, Graham, *Underground Graphics* (London: Academy Editions, 1970)

Kennedy, Garry Neill, *The Last Art College: Nova Scotia College of Art and Design, 1968–1978* (Cambridge, MA: MIT Press, 2012)

Khalfa, Jean, *The Dialogue Between Painting and Poetry: Livres D'Artistes 1874–1999* (Cambridge: Black Apollo Press, 2001)

Kholeif, Omar (ed.), *You Are Here: Art After the Internet* (London/Manchester: Space & Cornerhouse, 2014)

Kilgour, Frederick, *The Evolution of the Book* (New York, NY: Oxford University Press, 1998)

Kinmont, Ben, *Promised Relations: Or Second Thoughts Concerning a Few Artists' Contracts* (New York, NY: Antinomian Press, 1996)

Kinross, Robin, *Modern Typography: An Essay in Critical History* (London: Hyphen Press, 1992)

Kittler, Friedrich, Geoffrey Winthrop-Young and Michael Wutz (trans.), *Gramophone, Film, Typewriter* (Stanford, CA: Stanford University Press, 1999)

Klima, Stefan, *Artists' Books: A Critical Survey of the Literature* (New York, NY: Granary Books, 1998)

Kostelanetz, Richard, *Text: Found Texts* (New York, NY: William Morrow & Co., 1980)

Krajewski, Markus, Peter Krapp (trans.), *Paper Machines: About Cards and Catalogues, 1548–1929* (Cambridge, MA/London: MIT Press, 2011)

Krauss, Rolf H., *Beyond Light and Shadow* (Munich: Nazraeli Press, 1995)

Kubler, George, *The Shape of Time: Remarks on the History of Things* (New Haven, CT/London: Yale University Press, 1962)

Kuenzli, Rudolf, *Dada* (London: Phaidon Press, 2011)

Kugelberg, Johann and Jeremy Sanders, *Artists' Book Not Artists' Book* (New York, NY: Boo-Hooray & 6 Decades, 2012)

Kuhn, Alyson, *Art Made from Books: Altered, Sculpted, Carved, Transformed* (San Francisco, CA: Chronicle Books, 2013)

Lalou, Elisabeth, *Les Tablettes à Ecrire de l'Antiquité à l'Epoque Moderne, Actes du Colloque de Paris* (Turnhout: Brepols, 1992)

Lang, Anouk (ed.), *From Codex to Hypertext: Reading at the Turn of the Twenty-First Century* (Amherst, MA: University of Massachusetts Press, 2012)

Lanham, Richard A., *The Electronic World: Democracy, Technology, and the Arts* (Chicago, IL/London: University of Chicago Press, 1993)

Latour, Bruno, *An Inquiry into Modes of Existence: An Anthropology of the Moderns* (Cambridge, MA: Harvard University Press, 2013)

Leadbeater, Charles, *We-Think: Mass Innovation not Mass Production* (London: Profile, 2009)

Lecercle, Jean-Jacques, *Philosophy of Nonsense: The Intuitions of Victorian Nonsense Literature* (Abingdon: Taylor & Francis, 2002)

Lejeune, Denis, *The Radical Use of Chance in 20th Century Art* (Amsterdam: Rodopi Press, 2012)

Leppanen-Guerra, Analisa and Dickran Tashjian, *Joseph Cornell's Manual of Marvels* (London: Thames & Hudson, 2013)

Lessig, Lawrence, *Remix: Making Art and Commerce Thrive in the Digital Economy* (London: Penguin Books, 2009)

Lippard, Lucy, 'The Artists' Book Goes Public', *Art in America*, vol.65, no.1 January–February 1977

Loney, Alan, *The Books to Come* (Victoria, TX: Cuneiform Press, 2007)

——, *Meditatio: the printer printed: manifesto* (Victoria, TX: Cuneiform Press, 2004)

Lopez, Tony (ed.), *The Text Festivals: Language Art and Material Poetry* (Plymouth: University of Plymouth Press, 2013)

Loring, Rosamond A., *Marbled and Paste Papers: Rosamond Loring's Recipe Book* (Cambridge, MA: Houghton Library, Harvard, 2007)

——, *Decorated Book Papers* (Cambridge, MA: Houghton Library, Harvard, 2008)

Ludovico, Alessandro, *Post-Digital Print: The Mutation of Publishing Since 1894* (Eindhoven: Onomatopee, 2012)

Luhmann, Niklas, *Art as a Social System* (Stanford, CA: Stanford University, 2000)

Lupton, Ellen, *Thinking with Type: A Critical Guide for Designers, Writers, Editors and Students* (Princeton, NJ: Princeton Architectural Press, 2010)

Lyons, Joan (ed.), *Artists Books: A Critical Anthology and Sourcebook* (Rochester, NY: Visual Studies Workshop Press, 1985)

Lyons, Martin, *Books: A Living History* (London: Thames & Hudson, 2011)

Mabey, Richard, *Nature Cure* (London: Chatto & Windus, 2005)

Maffei, Giorgio, *Records by Artists 1958–1990* (Perugia/Ravenna: Viaindustriae Edizione & Danilo Montanari Editore, 2013)

Malpas, Jeff (ed.), *The Place of Landscape: Concepts, Contexts, Studies* (Cambridge, MA/London: MIT Press, 2011)

Manguel, Alberto, *The Library at Night* (New Haven, CT/London: Yale University Press, 2008)

Markov, Vladimir, *Russian Futurism: A History* (London: MacGibbon & Kee, 1969)

Matthews, George Tennyson, *News and Rumor in Renaissance Europe: The Fugger Newsletter* (New York, NY: Capricorn Books, 1959)

Mays, J. C. C., *Fredson Bowers and the Irish Wolfhound* (Clonmel: Coracle, 2002)

Mays, Sas (ed.), *Libraries, Literatures, and Archives* (Abingdon: Routledge, 2013)

McCloud, Scott, *Making Comics: Storytelling Secrets of Comics, Manga and Graphic Novels* (New York, NY: Harper Paperbacks, 2006)

McEwan, Indra Kagis, *Socrates' Ancestor* (Cambridge, MA/London: MIT Press, 1993)

McGann, Jerome, *Black Riders: the Visible Language of Modernism* (Princeton, NJ: Princeton University Press, 1993)

Meisse, Millard and Marcel Thomas, *The Rohan Master: A Book of Hours* (New York, NY: George Brazziller, 1973)

Mellor, David, *The Sixties Art Scene in London* (London: Phaidon Press, 1993)

Mise, Brandon, *Adventures in Letterpress* (London: Laurence King Publishers, 2014)

Mœglin-Delcroix, Anne, *Sur le Livre d'Artiste: Articles et Ecrits de Circonstance* 1981–2005 (Marseille: Le Mot et le Reste, 2006)

——, *Little Books and Other Little Publications* (Clonmel: Coracle, 2001)

——, *Livres d'Artistes: L'Invention d'un Genre 1960–1980* (Paris: Bibliothèque Nationale de France, 1997)

——, *Esthétique du Livre d'Artiste: 1960–1980* (Paris: Jean-Michel Place & Bibliothèque Nationale de France, 1997)

Monk, Geraldine, *Cusp: A Recollection of Poetry in Transition* (Bristol: Shearsman, 2012)

Montanaro, Ann R., *Pop-up and Movable Books: A Bibliography* (Metuchen, NJ: Scarecrow Press, 1993)

Morison, Stanley and Brooke Critchley (eds.), *A Tally of Types: With Additions by Several Hands* (Cambridge: Cambridge University Press, 1973)

Morley, C. L., *Xerography: An Annotated Bibliography* (Johannesburg: University of the Witwatersrand,1970)

Morris, Simon and Helen Sacoor, *Bibliomania* (York: Information as Material, 1998–99)

Morton, Timothy, *Hyperobjects: Philosophy and Ecology after the End of the World* (Minneapolis/St Paul, MN: University of Minnesota Press, 2013)

Muggeridge, Fraser and Sarah De Bondt (eds.), *The Form of the Book Book* (London: Occasional Papers, 2009)

Muggleton, David and Rupert Weinzieri (eds.), *The Post-Subcultures Reader* (Oxford: Berg, 2003)

Munari, Bruno, Patrick Creagh (trans.), *Design as Art* (London: Penguin Books, 1966)

——, *Original Xerographies* (Mantua: Edizioni Corraini, 2008)

Munby, A. N. L., Nicholas Barker (ed.), *Essays and Papers* (London: Scolar Press, 1977)

Myrone, Martin and Lucy Peltz (eds.), *Producing the Past: Aspects of Antiquarian Culture and Practice 1700–1850* (Aldershot: Ashgate, 1999)

Nagel, Alexander and Christopher Wood, *Anachronic Renaissance* (New York, NY: Zone Books, 2010)

Nancy, Jean-Luc, David Wills (trans.), *On the Commerce of Thinking: Of Books & Bookstores* (New York, NY: Fordham University Press, 2008)

Neurath, Marie and Robin Kinross, *The Transformer: Principles of Making Isotype Charts* (London: Hyphen Press, 2009)

Nuttall, Jeff, *Art and the Degradation of Awareness* (London: Calder, 1999)

Obrist, Hans Ulrich (ed.), *Mapping it Out: An Alternative Atlas of Contemporary Cartographies* (London: Thames & Hudson, 2014)

——, with Independent Curators International (eds.), *Do It: The Compendium* (New York, NY: DAP, 2013)

——, *Formulas for Now* (London: Thames & Hudson, 2008)

Ohrt, Robert (ed.), *Raymond Pettibon: The Books 1978–98* (New York, NY: Distributed Art Publishers, 2000)

Oldham, J. B., *Blind Panels of English Binders* (Cambridge: Cambridge University Press, 1958)

O'Neill, Alistair, *London After a Fashion* (London: Reaktion Books, 2007)

Ong, Walter J., *Orality and Literacy: Technologising the Word* (London/New York, NY: Methuen, 1982)

Osborne, Peter, *Anywhere or Not At All: Philosophy of Contemporary Art* (London/New York, NY: Verso, 2013)

Owen, Ted, *High Art: A History of the Psychedelic Poster* (London: Sanctuary Publishing, 1999)

Pächt, Otto, *Book Illumination in the Middle Ages: An Introduction* (London/Oxford: Harvey Miller & Oxford University Press, 1986)

Partington, Gill and Adam Smyth, *Book Destruction in the West: From the Medieval to the Contemporary* (Basingstoke: Palgrave Macmillan, 2014)

Perec, Georges and Simon Morris, *Species of Spaces and Other Pieces & Pigeon Reader* (Acklam: Information as Material, 2012)

Perloff, Marjorie, *The Futurist Moment: Avant-Garde, Avant Guerre, and the Language of Rupture* (Chicago, IL: University of Chicago Press, 2003)

——, *The Poetics of Indeterminacy: Rimbaud to Cage* (Princeton, NJ: Princeton University Press, 1981)

Perrée, Robert, *Cover to Cover: The Artist's Book in Perspective* (Rotterdam/Breda: NAI & De Beyerd, 2002)

Pettegree, Andrew, Paul Neave Nelles and Philip Conner (eds.), *The Sixteenth-Century French Religious Book* (Aldershot: Ashgate, 2001)

Phillpot, Clive, *Booktrek: Selected Essays on Artists' Books (1972–2010)* (Zurich/Dijon: JRP Ringier and Les Presses du Réel, 2013)

Piper, Andrew, *Book Was There: Reading in Electronic Times* (Chicago, IL: University of Chicago Press, 2012)

Pogarsky, Mikhail (ed.), *A Book about Artists' Books* (Moscow: Triangular Wheel, 2005)

Polanyi, Michael, *The Tacit Dimension* (New York, NY: Anchor Books, 1967)

Pomorska, Krystyna, *Russian Formalist Theory and its Poetic Ambience* (The Hague/Paris: Mouton, 1968)

Post van der Molen, Gerard, *De toekomst van ons grafisch verleden* (Amsterdam: De Stichting Drukwerk in de Marge, 2004)

Pritchard, Violet, *English Medieval Graffiti* (Cambridge: Cambridge University Press, 2008)

Puttenham, George, *The Arte of Englishe Poesie* (London: Richard Field, 1585)

Rafaeli, Ari, *Book Typography* (London/New Castle, DE: The British Library & Oak Knoll Press, 2005)

Ratcliff, Carter, *Out of the Box: The Reinvention of Art, 1965–1975* (New York, NY: Allworth Press, 2000)

Raza, Naheed (ed.), *Ravelling, Unravelling* (London: Wellcome Trust, 2009)

Relyea, Lane, Your *Everyday Art World* (Cambridge, MA/London: MIT Press, 2013)

Rhein, Donna E., *The Handprinted Books of Leonard and Virginia Woolf at the Hogarth Press, 1917–1932* (Ann Arbour, MI/Epping: UMI Research, Bowker, c.1985)

Richard, Sophie and Lynda Morris (ed.), *Unconcealed, the International Network of Conceptual Artists 1967–77: Dealers, Exhibitions and Public Collections* (London: Ridinghouse, 2009)

Richardson, Bob, *The Adana Connection* (London: British Printing Society, 1997)

Richie, Ward, *A Guide to the Hand Press* (Wakefield: Fleece Press, c.1989)

Richter, Hans, *Dada: Art and Anti-Art* (London: Thames & Hudson, 1997)

Riddell, Alan, *Typewriter Art* (London: London Magazine Editions, 1975)

Ridgeway, Renée and Katarina Zdjelar, *Another Publication* (Rotterdam/Frankfurt am Main: Piet Zwart Institute & Revolver, 2007)

Robinson, Edward S., *Shift Linguals: Cut-Up Narratives from William S. Burroughs to the Present Day* (Amsterdam/New York, NY: Rodopi, 2011)

Rogers, Martin and Simon Cutts (eds.), *The Printed Performance: Brian Lane, Works 1966–99* (Derby: RGAP, 2001)

Rosen, Margaret (ed.), *A Little-Known Story about a Movement, a Magazine and the Computer's Arrival in Art: New Tendencies and Bit International, 1961–1973* (Cambridge, MA/London: MIT Press, 2011)

Rosenberg, Harold, *The Anxious Object* (New York, NY: Horizon Press, 1966)

Rota, Anthony, *Apart from the Text* (Pinner, Middlesex/New Castle, DE: Private Libraries Association & Oak Knoll Press, 1999)

Rowell, Margit and Deborah Wye, Joanne Greenspun (ed.), *The Russian Avant-Garde Book 1910–1934* (New York: MOMA, 2002)

Rummonds, Richard-Gabriel, *Printing on the Iron Handpress* (London/New Castle, DE: The British Library & Oak Knoll Press, 1998)

Sackett, Colin, *Englshpublshing: Writing and Readings 1991–2002* (Clonmel/Limoges/Exeter: Coracle, Sixtus, Spacex, 2004)

Sampson, Tony D., *Virality: Contagion Theory in the Age of Networks* (Minneapolis, MN: University of Minnesota Press, 2012)

Sansi, Roger, Art, *Anthropology and the Gift* (London: Bloomsbury Academic, 2014)

Sansom, Ian, *Paper: An Elegy* (London: Fourth Estate, 2012)

Saper, Craig, *Networked Art* (Minneapolis, MN: University of Minnesota Press, 2001)

Scanlan, John, *On Garbage* (London: Reaktion Books, 2004)

Scherer, Jacques, *Le "Livre" de Mallarmé* (Paris: Gallimard, 1957)

Schlesinger, Kyle, *Poems & Pictures: A Renaissance in the Art of the Book 1946–1981* (New York, NY: Center for Book Arts, 2010)

Schmidt, Gunnar, *Klavierzerstörungen in Kunst und Popkultur* (Reimer Verlag, Berlin: 2012)

Schmoller, Tanya (intro.), *In Praise of Patterned Papers: A Collection of Essays* (Oldham: Incline, 1997)

Scholderer, Victor, *Johann Gutenberg: the Inventor of Printing* (London: British Museum, 1963)

Schwartz, Hillel, *Making Noise: From Babel to the Big Bang and Beyond* (Cambridge, MA: Zone Books, 2011)

——, *The Culture of the Copy: Striking Likenesses, Unreasonable Facsimiles* (Cambridge, MA: Zone Books, 1998)

Sennett, Richard, *The Craftsman* (London: Allen Lane, 2008)

Shaughnessy, Adrian, *Essays: Scratching the Surface* (London: Unit 13, 2013)

——, *F. A. K. Henrion: The Complete Designer* (London: Unit 13, 2013)

Shaw, Henry, *Alphabets, Numerals and Devices of the Middle Ages* (London: Pickering, 1845)

Sherman, William H., *Used Books: Marking Readers in Renaissance England* (Philadelphia, PA: University of Pennsylvania Press, 2010)

Shumaker, Wayne, *The Occult Sciences in the Renaissance* (Oakland, CA: University of California Press, 2009)

Siegenthaler, Fred, *Strange Papers: A Collection of the World's Rarest Handmade Papers* (Muttenz: Paper Art, 1987)

Šindelář, Dušan, *Tržiště Estetiky* (Prague: Obelisk, 1969)

Singh, Simon, *The Code Book: The Science of Secrecy from Ancient Egypt to Quantum Cryptography* (New York, NY: Anchor, 2000)

Sloman, Paul (ed.), *Paper: Tear, Fold, Rip, Crease, Cut* (London: Black Dog, 2009)

Small, Ian and Marcus Walsh, *The Theory and Practice of Text-Editing* (Cambridge: Cambridge University Press, 1992)

Smith, Keith A., *Two Hundred Books: An Annotated Bibliography* (Rochester: Keith A. Smith Books, 2000)

Smith, Margaret M., *The Title Page: Its Early Development 1460–1510* (London/New Castle, DE: The British Library & Oak Knoll Press, 2000)

Smith, Philip, *The Book as Art and Object* (Merstham: Paul Smith, 1982)

Smith, Terry, *What is Contemporary Art?* (Chicago, IL: University of Chicago Press, 2009)

Smitshuijzen, Edo, *Signage Design Manual* (Zurich: Lars Müller, 2007)

Sparrow, John, *Visible Words: A Study of Inscriptions in and as Books and Works of Art* (Cambridge: Cambridge University Press, 1969)

Spector, Buzz, *Buzzwords* (Chicago, IL: Sara Ranchouse Publishing, 2012)

——, *The Bookmaker's Desire: Writings on the Art of the Book* (Pasadena, CA: Umbrella Associates, 1995)

Spieker, Sven, *The Big Archive* (Cambridge, MA/London: MIT Press, 2008)

Spoerri, Daniel, et al, Malcom Green (trans.), *An Anecdoted Topography of Chance* (London: Atlas Press, 1995)

Stagl, Justin, *A History of Curiosity: The Theory of Travel, 1550–1800* (Amsterdam: Harwood Academic Publishers, 1995)

Steeds, Lucy et al, *Making Art Global (Part 2): 'Magiciens de la Terre' 1989* (London: Afterall Books, 2014)

Stein, Jeannine, *Re-Bound: Creating Handmade Books from Recycled and Repurposed Materials* (Minneapolis, MN: Quarry Books, 2009)

Steinberg S. H., John Trevitt (revision), *Five Hundred Years of Printing* (London/New Castle, DE: The British Library & Oak Knoll Press, 2001)

Stewart, Garrett, *Bookwork: Medium to Object to Concept to Art* (Chicago, IL: University of Chicago Press, 2011)

Strasser, Susan, *Waste and Want: A Social History of Trash* (New York, NY; Metropolitan Books, 1999)

Talbot, William Henry Fox, *The Pencil of Nature* (London: Mapp, 2013)*

Thompson, Jason, *Playing with Books: The Art of Upcycling, Deconstructing, and Reimagining the Book* (Minneapolis, MI: Quarry Book, 2010)

Tollbeek, Jo and Eline van Assche (eds.), *Ravaged: Art and Culture in Times of Conflict* (New Haven, CT: Yale University Press, 2014)

Tooley, Ronald Vere, *English Books with Coloured Plates, 1790 to 1860: A Bibliographical Account of the Most Important Books Illustrated by English Artists in Colour Aquatint and Colour Lithography* (London: Batsford, 1954)

Tourtillott Suzanne J. E. (ed.), *500 Handmade Books: Inspiring Interpretations of a Timeless Form* (New York, NY: Lark Books, 2008)

Tuer, Andrew W., *Pages and Pictures from Forgotten Children's Books* (London: The Leadenhall Press Ltd., 1898–9)

Tullett, Barrie (ed.), *Typewriter Art: A Modern Anthology* (London: Laurence King Publishing, 2014)

Turner, Silvie (ed.), *Facing the Page: British Artists' Books: A Survey 1983–1993* (London: Estamp, 1993)

TwoPoints.net, *Left, Right, Up, Down: New Directions in Signage and Wayfinding* (Berlin: Gestalten Verlag, 2010)

Van Den Bergh, George, *Capital Letters, Twin and Multiple Print* (Haarlem: Tjeenk Willink and Sons, 1958)

Van Der Weel, Adrian, *Changing Our Textual Minds* (Manchester: University of Manchester Press, 2011)

Vergine, Lea, *When Trash Becomes Art: Trash Rubbish Mongo* (Milan: Skira, 2007)

——, *Art on the Cutting Edge: A Guide to Contemporary Movements* (Milan: Skira, 2001)

Volta, Ornella (ed.), Antony Melville (trans.), *A Mammal's Notebook: The Writings of Erik Satie* (London: Atlas Press, 2014)

Waeckerlé, Emmanuelle and Richard Sawdon Smith (eds.), *The Book is Alive!* (Sheffield: RGAP, 2013)

Walser, Robert, Susan Bernofsky (trans.), *Microscripts* (New York, NY: Christine Burgin Gallery, 2012)

Walker, John A., *John Latham: The Incidental Person: His Art and Ideas* (London: Middlesex University Press, 1994)

Ward, James, *Adventures in Stationery: A Journey Through Your Pencil Case* (London: Profile Books, 2014)

Warburg, Aby M., *Mnemosyne: Atlas* (Madrid: Akal Ediciones, 2010)

Warnke, Martin (ed.), *Der Bilderatlas Mnemosyne* (Berlin: Akademie Verlag, 2012)

Wassermann, Krystyna, *The Book as Art: Books from the National Museum of Women in the Arts* (New York, NY: Princeton Architectural Press, 2011)

Weber, Carl J., *A Thousand and One Fore-Edge Paintings: With Notes on the Artists, Bookbinders, Publishers and Other Men and Women Connected with the History of a Curious Art* (Waterville, ME: Colby College Press, 1949)

Wechsler, Dan (ed.), *Strange & Wonderful: An Informal Visual History of Manuscript Books and Albums* (New York, NY: Sanctuary Publishing, 2010)

Weiss Alan S., *Shattered Forms: Art Brut, Phantasms, Modernism* (Albany, NY: State University of New York Press, 1992)

Wesseling, Janneke (ed.), *See It Again, Say It Again: The Artist as Researcher* (Amsterdam: Valiz, 2011)

Wieck, Roger S., *Time Sanctified: The Book of Hours in Medieval Art and Life* (New York, NY: George Braziller, 2001)

Wiles, H. V., *The Horn-Book: The First Rung on the Ladder of Literacy* (Eastbourne: Whale-back, 2010)

Willberg, Hans Peter and Friedrich Forssmann, *Lesetypographie* (Mainz: Verlag Hermann Schmidt, 2005)

Williamson, Hugh, *Methods of Book Design: The Practice of an Industrial Craft* (London: Oxford University Press, 1966)

Wiseman, Susan, *Writing Metamorphosis in the English Renaissance 1550–1700* (Cambridge: Cambridge University Press, 2014)

Wittgenstein, Ludwig, *Philosophical Investigations* (Blackwell: Oxford, 1953)

Wohlrab, Lutz (ed.), *Robert Rehfeldt: Kunst im Kontakt* (Berlin: Wohlrab Verlag, 2009)

Wright, Maggie, *All You Need to Know About Rubber Stamping* (Tunbridge Wells: Search Press, 1995)

Young, La Monte, *An Anthology of Chance Operations etc* (New York, NY: Young & Jackson Mac Low, 1963)

Young, Sherman, *The Book is Dead: Long Live the Book* (Sydney: University of New South Wales, 2007)

Zambelli, Paola, *White Magic, Black Magic in the European Renaissance* (Leiden: Brill, 2007)

Zeegan, Lawrence, *Ladybird by Design* (London: Ladybird Books, 2015)

Zoller, Rahel, *The Inner Monologue of a Book* (London: Self-Published, 2012)

* App or ebook

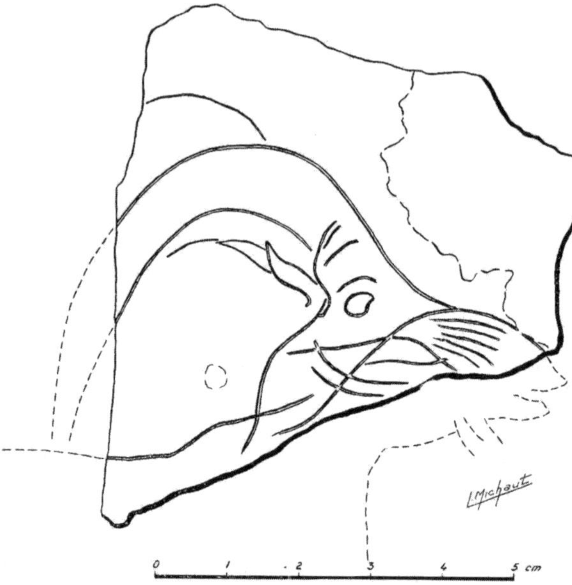

Thanks are due to the following: John Bevis, Sarah Bodman, Victoria Browne, Luisa Calè, Ami Clarke, Simon Cutts, EC, Ailsa Ferrier, Ajay Hothi, Deeqa Ismail, Elizabeth James, Gill Partington, Mikhail Pogarsky, Rare Books & Music at The British Library, Bethan Sackett-Thomas, Tate Library, Emmanuelle Waeckerlé and Thom Winterburn, who in their various ways have aided and abetted this project; and Colin Sackett, who both as editor and designer has nudged me along, excised my less fortunate articulations, and oversaw the completion of this book.

INDEX OF NAMES

Pages A–Z refer to 'Exposé', between p.70 and p.97.